Edge of the Map

Edge of the Map

One Year in a Closed Country

Pilgrim Tyne

RESOURCE *Publications* · Eugene, Oregon

EDGE OF THE MAP
One Year in a Closed Country

Resource Publications
An Imprint of Wipf and Stock Publishers
199 W. 8th Ave., Suite 3
Eugene, OR 97401

www.wipfandstock.com

ISBN 13: 978-1-62564-287-5

Manufactured in the U.S.A.

To the unnamed souls in this book,
with whom I continue to find my way.

Contents

Introduction   *xi*

PART ONE: Calling

one   Reconciling Shadows   3

two   Discontent vs. Apathy   11

three   Definition   19

four   Opposition   27

five   Walking Through a Door   33

PART TWO: Adjustment

six   A Torch in the Fog   43

seven   Our New Body   51

eight   Successes and Failures . . . Mostly Failures   59

nine   Unchecked Baggage   67

ten   Slow Walks   73

PART THREE: Incubation

eleven   The Trough   81

twelve   City Relics   89

thirteen   The Comfortable Lie   95

fourteen   Evening Tea   101

fifteen   Deterioration   107

PART FOUR: Grace

sixteen   Phoenix   115

seventeen   Resolved   123

Acknowledgements   127

Bibliography   129

Introduction

I can't tell you my name.
I can't tell you where I live.
I can't tell you who I work for, or any details about the people with whom I work.
Because where I live, my line of work is not exactly legal.
But if you can pardon the vague, I have a story for you.

PART ONE

Calling

one

Reconciling Shadows

"Show me where we're going, Daddy."

My two-year-old daughter pointed to a giant wall map in the foyer of my father's church—the kind with a slight grade in its topography, so the mountains seem to come out at you from the wall. My daughter, still grappling with the concept of the earth and its oceans and land masses, stood mesmerized.

"Hmm, let's see." I picked her up and we inspected the map more closely together.

My father's church was not ignorant of the world, and in fact had become more focused on international partnerships with each passing year. This mindset, however, had yet to find its way to the wall map, which depicted North America in its centered, prominent place, and split the other side of the world in half down the middle.

"Well, right now we live here," I said, pointing to the dead center of the map. "But in a few weeks we're moving here . . ." I searched the map for our destination, first one half of the fractured biosphere, and then the other. My daughter watched my befuddled finger stroke the air.

I couldn't find our city on the map because it wasn't there. In fact, almost our entire country had been erased in this tragically framed picture of the world.

I touched the edge of the map, and then moved my finger a few inches beyond its polished wooden frame.

"Here."

"It's not even on the map?"

"Well, it's not on this map, but it's there."

"Are you sure?"

"I'm pretty sure."

"Ok, Dad."

Less than one month later I stood on the corner of a densely crowded street, fifty pounds of groceries hanging from my shoulders, my daughter in one arm, a city map in the other, trying unsuccessfully to hail a taxi with my outstretched neck. The dark and the chaos of noise and the deficit of personal space all merged, stifling our capacity for breath. Across the street, a pack of firecrackers burst to life and my daughter trembled at the sound as she clutched my neck. She hid her face from the noise and the smells and the oncoming headlights. I felt my arms stiffening and wondered how long I would be able to stand on that street corner holding her. I felt a deep breath of polluted air passing through my nose and wondered how many years it was shaving from my life. I felt my shoulders sag and wondered, as I had only a few times in my life, whether I had, in fact, made a terrible mistake.

Almost all of the taxis rushed past us already occupied. The ones that weren't didn't stop either. I watched them sail by like escape pods that might have been, powerless to rescue myself or my daughter from the stultifying street corner.

Then a taxi slowed as it came around the corner and mercifully pulled up right in front of me. I elbowed my way through the other pedestrians to its passenger side, waited for the current occupant to exit, then locked eyes with the driver.

"Foreign Language University?" I offered.

"Huh?" He furrowed his brow.

I tried one more time in English, but when he clearly didn't understand, I tried in the local language, doing my best to pronounce the words the way I'd been taught.

The driver's face wrinkled even further. He said a string of words I couldn't make out, but by his tone I assumed them to be the rough equivalent of, "What the heck are you trying to say?"

"Please," I said. "I just need to get back to Foreign Language University." My body bent under the weight of the bags and my child and the dark night. I begged him, with my face, to understand.

He looked at me, not unkindly, but then he waved us away with the back of his hand and drove up a few meters to another pack of potential occupants—passengers less burdened, who could speak the language, who knew where they were going—a much easier fare.

After failing to adequately communicate my desired destination to four separate taxis drivers, I had the idea to call my contact at the university. When a fifth taxi finally stopped for us, my contact correctly pronounced the name of our school over my newly purchased cell phone. The driver smiled as we climbed in with all our bags.

He asked me a question I couldn't comprehend.

I just shrugged my heavy shoulders.

He laughed good-naturedly and I tried not to feel like he was making fun of me. My daughter relaxed a little in my lap. At least we were heading home. Sort of home.

I thought if I knew where the school was on the map I could point it out to future taxi drivers, but the map was not in English. When we stopped at a traffic light I held the map up to the driver and used body language and facial expressions to try to elicit the school's location. He frowned for a moment, then understood, and began to search the map with me. I watched his finger hover above the map, unsure. Finally, he pointed about an inch above where the map cut off.

"Here?" I asked.

He nodded.

"It's not even on the map?"

The light changed and he looked away from my question to focus on the road.

I let my useless map fall to the floor of the taxi. I shut my eyes to the blur of lights passing outside the window. The lights illuminated faces, and the faces all seemed angry. I rolled up the window to drown out the noise. My trip to the store was supposed to have taken an hour or two. We'd easily been gone six. My daughter had missed dinner. My wife, who didn't have a cell phone yet, was probably out of her mind with worry. I tried to shut my eyes to all of that, and to look inside for that stillness, that surety, but I couldn't find it.

For the duration of the ride I tried to relocate my sanity, and I did this by recounting the journey that had brought my family and me to this country. Where had we been, and what had prompted the change? How had we gotten here? When had I ever had time to notice that tender place in my heart, and how could I have been so foolish as to yield to it?

In other words: why did we say yes?

You should know at the outset that I never planned to be a missionary. I'm sure some people do. I never did.

I took a few short-term trips, and I can truthfully call them times of genuine spiritual formation. They introduced me to themes and concepts that became important paths to sojourn. They impacted me, certainly, but not with the kind of force that catalyzes a family to move overseas.

When I was young and missionaries came to our church, it was always apparent to me that they belonged to some other class of heavenly citizen. On two counts, primarily.

First of all, they had an incredible zeal for evangelism. When they talked about the gospel it was as if speaking those words was what they were made by the creator to do. Passion bled from their eyes and sang from their lips, and their bodies visibly shook as they told the story. Quite simply, they loved telling others about Jesus.

Evangelism doesn't come naturally to me. I do tremble when I share the gospel, but more from nerves than enthusiasm. I get distracted thinking about the magnitude of the moment—pondering how it was ordained by the creator of the universe and whatnot—and I start to lose track of what I'm saying. I leave out important parts of the gospel and repeat inconsequential elements over and over. I start to sweat a lot, wondering if my testimony and presentation is actually distancing others from Jesus rather than drawing them close—like I might actually have negative gifts in evangelism. Sharing my faith makes me nervous, and when I attempt to do it, it's not a pretty sight.

Secondly, the missionaries I met were always so fervent about their target people group. I could see it in their eyes: they loved East Africans more than they loved Americans. They wept as they told stories of hardships or joys, their lives so entwined with their friends in the field. They absorbed their host culture to such a degree that they felt like foreigners in the towns where they grew up. They dressed like a running joke but were never themselves in on it, indirectly mocking us with their choice to abandon the very things we held dear, like fast-food and television.

I didn't have anything against East Africans per se, but I definitely didn't love them. In fact, I didn't love anyone like these heroes of God seemed to love others.

So, on account of how I was clearly "o and 2" on both requirements, I considered myself exempt from anything like a missionary calling, and I felt as though God had no business asking me to serve him overseas.

God says that his strength is made perfect in our weakness, and that when we are weak, we are strong.[1] God says that he has chosen the foolish things of the world to confound the wise, and the weak things of the world to overcome the strong.[2]

But I didn't understand any of that yet.

I like to take walks by myself, but usually during the daylight, because walking alone in the dark is rarely a pleasure. It usually involves a lot of magnified noises, darting eyes and quickened steps. When I walk beneath a dim streetlight, the multiple shadows cast by my hurried cadence leap to catch me like a gang of assailants. A shiver runs from my scalp to my fingertips, stiffening and then

1. 2 Cor 12:9–10.
2. 1 Cor 1:27.

releasing me in a breath. It's frightening, but in that same adrenal moment all of my shadows converge into a single outline—a crisp silhouette. I rarely pause long enough to see it though, because I'm too afraid of what I'll see.

How often in this life have I found myself running from the shadows I cast—afraid of my influence, uncertain of the impression I broadcast to the world? How often do I let myself move to that place of clarity, reconciling shadows in my wake, only to blink and miss the image and still have no idea who I really am?

To put it another way, does such a thing as "calling" exist?

Of course, one usually has to be alone in the dark in order to happen upon such opportunities for clarity. But everyone is alone, in a way. And dark, it certainly is.

About the time I started noticing the tender place in my heart that would weaken and spread until it eventually caved in and gave way to a calling, I read a story in the news that made me regret being a part of the human race, as the news often does. The story was about a teenager who was raped in a parking lot during a school dance. She was an outcast among her peers, and her classmates stood by just out of view, snapping photos with their cell phones.

It made me wonder how God continues to put up with us, and why. We are all, the lot of us, cruel and deserving of death—whether we rape a teenager in a parking lot, or just stand by and witness it without protest. We have such a deep capacity for horrible things. I weep when I think of this story—for the girl, for her parents, for the rapists and the watchers, and for myself, because I am no better. I'm a part of it, too.

We live in a dark place.

I think every human being, on some level, wrestles with that.

So, when I walk down the street at night, while I can't really control the shape or the color or the intensity of the light through which I'm cast, I can to an extent contort my frame to influence the shadows I make: shadows of blessing, for instance, rather than cursing; kindness rather than cruelty. Such contortions often come off like a mad batch of flailing about, but there is a stirring in me that says I at least ought to try.

That desire, to take ownership of my effect on the world, was what prompted me to listen for a call upon my life.

It is a weighty blessing and responsibility, this Christian truth that we all matter. I want to live in such a way that when those moments arise, in which all my shadows reconcile, I won't be found timidly running from a vapid threat, or self-consciously shrinking from what surrounds, but instead, eyes forward, confident that who I am can dictate what I do, and that if I focus on my soul I will not regret it.

This is the nature of life lived at the edge of the map.

two

Discontent vs. Apathy

I HAD A NUMBER of good excuses to ignore my ringing cell phone. I'd slid a good thirty minutes into that post-lunch coma—which the civilized world acknowledges with an appropriate siesta, but which we Americans feel compelled to work through—so I had to pull my eyes away from reading and re-reading the lines of a work-related email to even notice the call. I had a meeting coming up, for which I was not prepared, and my body was fighting an illness that had already worked its way through my wife and daughter. But since the ringing phone was also a kind of salvation from the monotony of the office, I answered.

I ended up being late for my meeting.

My wife was in tears on the other end of the line, which of course prompted my brain to play out a string of doomsday scenarios in the time it took her to catch her breath. Despite my considerable imagination, her first words still shocked me.

"You were right," she said.

I belong to the camp of husbands who are not privileged to hear these words from a spouse on any kind of basis that might be called regular. I had no idea what I was right about, or why it had brought my wife to tears, but I congratulated myself for having been right about something, and for having picked up the phone to find out about it.

"You were right," she said. "We're supposed to go."

My wife had been holding our fourteen-month-old baby in her arms the first time I suggested to her that we seriously consider moving to the 10/40 window now—not later, not when our kids were grown, not in the twilight years of our retirement. Now.

Her response had gone something like, "Hmm . . . that's nice," her estimation of my idiocy apparent between the lines.

I asked her to pray about it.

She agreed in a way that made clear to me she had no intention of praying about it.

That was two weeks before the phone call. During those two weeks she'd been feeling little nudges, hints that perhaps she should indeed pray about it, most of which she ignored. But that afternoon she had finally consented to ask God for direction. She asked him if we should go, and he answered.

I took my cell phone outside and walked around my office building a few times while she told me about her conversation with God. Through tears she read me the passages of the Bible to which she had been drawn. She read them completely out of context and with utter disregard for exegetical method—exactly opposite to the way she'd been taught in Bible school—but with confidence that the Holy Spirit was quickening her own spirit with the words on the page. When she was finished reading, she was certain that God had spoken directly to her heart.

Her tears were half from fear, half from the painful thoughts of leaving family behind, and half from the sweet reverence that swells when the God of the universe takes time to speak to his children. She was 150 percent convinced that our family should begin exploring options overseas.

Later, when things got hard, I had to remind her of this moment, so she would remember it wasn't all my fault.

We in the Christian community tend to speak of calling in a generic sort of way. "We're all called to this or that," we say. This is not necessarily a bad way to approach a conversation about faith, as indeed there are things that every person in a genuine pursuit of Jesus must take up. These are the things that unite us; our common purposes.

But a vague definition of calling is also a disservice to a generation of young people hungry to devote themselves to God. "How do I know that, or to what, I am called?" they will ask. Their dreams for God are so easily obscured by questions about the nature of calling. Will my phone literally ring? Will I hear an audible voice? Will my circumstances magically align? Should I go even if they don't align?

I won't speak on the totality of what a Christian calling means, or even a specifically "missionary" calling, but I will tell you what it looked like for us.

For us, it came in stages.

I have a tall friend named Jason who plays the guitar. When anybody talks to Jason about how they don't hear from God anymore, Jason asks in a very casual way, "What was the last thing God told you to do? Did you do it?"

Sometimes God hasn't given us a new direction because he is still waiting for us to obey the last thing he said. God is patient like that.

When we started to sense a calling, my wife and I were already involved in ministry. In fact, I feel comfortable adding the modifier "heavily" to that statement. During our first five years of marriage we both led multiple ministries at our church at one time or another. My wife taught at a Christian school before our daughter was born. My job on a local university campus was also what you would probably call full-time ministry.

We were serving God. We were tilling the soil with our hands to the plow, and we were bearing some fruit, personally and in ministry.

But we weren't satisfied.

I don't mean to say that we weren't grateful. I look back on those five years and remember how privileged we felt. Now and again our hearts would be stirred for something overseas, but we took those stirrings and used them as fuel for the present work God had set before us. We did that for as long as we could. Around the five-year mark, things were unraveling.

That isn't to say our ministries had quite grown stale (though that was occasionally what it felt like). We loved our church and we loved the work we were doing. We fought to be sincere in our efforts, and repented if we caught ourselves just going through the motions. We did our best. But month by month it became clear to us that we were simply unfulfilled. We were hungry for God in a way we couldn't define, like part of our spiritual appetite was going unmet, and it was slowly driving us mad.

Some people like to blame their pastors or their bosses or their parents for this lack of satisfaction. But in our case it was no-one's fault. It was simply a precursor to calling.

Dissatisfaction is tricky because it isn't always evidence of calling. We are fallen creatures after all. Sometimes we just want more. Sometimes we're dissatisfied with what God has put in front of us because everything seems to be going wrong. Sometimes we ought to suck it up, obey, and wait for the Spirit to produce joy in us. But sometimes everything seems to be going right, yet we remain discontent. That's when we ought to ask ourselves if the source of our restlessness may in fact be that we are not doing what God has called us to do.

Sometimes dissatisfaction is the finger of God, pointing to something more.

Then again, sometimes we don't care about anything more.

I know we're supposed to hunger and thirst for righteousness, and I sincerely want to want that. I long for a deeper capacity to do what is pleasing to the Lord and for good works. I want to be satisfied in him alone. But do you know what I hunger and thirst for even more than that?

Entertainment.

Around the same time I was wrestling with all these feelings of discontent—perhaps because of them—I was essentially planning my week around the television schedule. I had a late-night routine of shows to watch, and I planned my lunch breaks around getting caught up on the shows I missed. I'd get convicted about it for a while, and try to limit my intake, but even when I cut back to just a few shows a week I was no less wrapped up in them. I looked forward to them and thought about them such that they became the highlight of my day.

There's only one word for it: idolatry.

Don't hear me bemoaning the horrors of entertainment because I don't think TV is always bad. I just think we shouldn't love it too much. And unfortunately it is not as easy as just unplugging the flat screen. Distraction is like a shell game—something else will always come up.

The solution is to pursue Christ. To seek him so much that to seek him becomes the best part of our day. We don't have to manufacture attraction because in his face all else fades. We just need to look at him.

A distracted people are a people prone to apathy.

As I struggled with this apathetic attitude, watching the seconds of my life flutter away like flecks of paint on a dying house, I read the gospel of Mark and noticed something I hadn't noticed before. I read the opening chapter, in which Jesus famously says to the men who would become his disciples, "Follow me, and I will make you become fishers of men."[1] I had heard this expression many times without realizing the reference Jesus actually made with those words.

I turned to the passage in Jeremiah 16, which is a more haunting picture, but no less hopeful. God declares that he will call for hunters and fishers to catch up his chosen people and return them to their rightful place. But he is also calling them back from sin. He says, "They have polluted my land with the carcasses of their detestable idols, and have filled my inheritance with their abominations."[2] Then the prophet cries out, "To you shall the nations come from the ends of the earth and say: 'Our fathers have inherited nothing but lies, worthless things in which there is no profit.'"[3]

1. Mark 1:17 ESV.
2. Jer 16:18b ESV.
3. Jer 16:19b ESV.

These words clung to me. They called out the severe connection between this missional call and the displacing of idols. They cut me with deep conviction.

In the West our idols don't stink like rotting carcasses. They are much more subtle than that, but they make us just as unclean, and they make us apathetic to real life. They distract us from the calling we might otherwise be about. We have the idea that missionaries ought to be the ones who channel the light, and bring ruin to the altars of pagan gods in foreign lands, but there is another battle with idolatry, a more personal battle, that must also take place if we are to answer a call.

Somewhere along this taut line of tension between discontent and apathy was where we found ourselves in November of 2009. At that time I was very mindful of the lines from Proverbs, "Keep deception and lies far from me, give me neither poverty nor riches; feed me with the food that is my portion, that I not be full and deny You and say, 'Who is the Lord?' Or that I not be in want and steal, and profane the name of my God."[4]

Was our dissatisfaction somehow a nudge from God, or were we just living in apathetic sin? It seemed trivial to reduce it like this, but at the time there was a very subtle and daily war being waged over whether or not we would hear the call and respond. Some days we fasted and prayed, some days we just watched TV. Every day God was faithful.

We began to feel the weight of this tension, like the warm thickness in the air before a hurricane sets in. Our daughter started suffering from intense fevers. We felt uneasy in our home, like a hungry lion might be waiting just on the other side of the thin walls. My wife and I were both woken in the night to pray with urgency for unknown requests.

This was essentially the first stage of our calling—not specific as to location, ministry or sending agency. It was only this question:

4. Prov 30:8–9 NASB.

Were we willing to leave? Our initial answer to the question was somewhere between discontent and apathy.

Then it got serious. My wife told her parents.

I was out of town for work when she sprung the news on them that we were thinking of making a change. It went about as bad as it could possibly go. They lambasted her with dozens of things that could go wrong, including a list of diseases that would likely claim our lives and the life of our daughter, without seeming to hear to her appeal. They regaled her with fantastic—borderline fictitious—tales of the horrors of life abroad. They said it was a terrible, irresponsible idea, and their argument ended with our daughter being kidnapped and sold into slavery.

I got another tear-filled phone call.

I should mention that my mother- and father-in-law are wonderfully sweet people, who treat me and my family very well. And they also happen to be Christians. They just weren't ready for us to answer a call overseas. Parents rarely are.

There were a number of readily available excuses floating around at that time, and a great deal of uncertainty, but the question itself was a simple one: Were we willing to leave? I was adamant with the desire to not use my child as justification to refuse a call. I imagined sitting down on the couch with an eighteen-year-old version of my daughter and telling her to her face, "God told us to go, but we stayed because of you." How could we do that? And if we wouldn't say it to her face, neither could we live like it was true. The responsibility was not fit for her shoulders.

The choice was neither our parents' nor our daughter's to make. It belonged to us.

Convictions like these were one of the ways God spoke to us during this stage of our calling. Through his Word he breathed into the tension of our lives, a fragrance both heavy and enticing. He spoke to us through the hunger of our hearts and he gently illustrated the appetites that had grown into moss-covered idols. He moved like a mist into the chaotic space we occupied, and we tried to keep walking with our arms out in front of us, but it was useless to keep moving forward. We had to stop. The only clear thing was the question we knew he wanted us to answer: Were we willing to leave?

This stage was intense, and frankly, quite messy. We had no idea where he was calling us to go, but eventually we were able to answer him honestly: Yes, we'll go.

We answered that question in November of 2009, only a few weeks before the Urbana conference.

three

Definition

IT WASN'T MY SHIFT to drive the van, so I leaned into my seat watching trees in various stages of rebirth flash by the passenger window like oversized faces from my past—like a kind of Mt. Rushmore in motion before stratus clouds of my subconscious. I was en-route to St. Louis with a group of students, hoping that God would shed a bit of light on my future, and thinking about the future often brings up the past.

I've never had a long-term master plan for the course of my life, and I don't think most of us do. Life comes in stages, one season giving way to the next, and it has been my experience that a life laid down for God will find each new phase somehow contingent upon those that came before.

The "youth group" season prepared me for leadership roles in college, which also helped to direct my course of study, which in turn helped prepare me for my first job, and so on.

It seems to me that God is always doing this—always shaping us through tangibles and intangibles, priming us for something else, and it's not until we arrive at the next stage that we can look back and see how all our experience, all of our seasons, have converged to prepare us.

I took my first mission trip less than a year after I believed and began to follow Jesus. It was the summer between my sophomore and junior year of high school and I went with twenty-three other young people whom I had never met to a country in the 10/40 window that floods in the summertime. We lived there for almost four weeks, and our "work" changed a lot, but the eventual task settled on by our leaders was to build a school in a small village (easier said than done when the rain never stopped). We were very headstrong and task oriented, as young Americans typically are, and I remember my chagrin at sitting around watching the rain, accomplishing nothing. I remember that for much of the trip I felt like we were wasting time.

Up to that point I had never heard the phrase "incarnational ministry" (and if I had, I would have assumed it had something to do with outreach to cannibals). Near the end of our time overseas it became apparent that a number of nationals were somewhat troubled by our presence in the village. When we worked up the courage to ask them about it they said it wasn't because we had done anything wrong, they just didn't understand us. Why would a group of high school students, Americans, give up a summer to come to their village? They couldn't figure it out.

I'm familiar with most of the arguments for and against short-term mission trips, and I tend to think each side has a valid argument. I believe in accountability and long-term relationships, and I have first-hand experience of the damage teams can cause, but I've also witnessed deep measures of blessing, on both sides. I still believe that short-term teams can be powerful, if they are done well.

I got my first intestinal parasite on that short-term mission trip. Some days I used the squatty—occupied by a nest of hornets—on an hourly basis. I got ringworm for the first time, I lost about twenty pounds of video game fat, I made a lot of friends, and I learned a lot about God. But the biggest lesson I learned was about presence. Whether or not we built a school in that village was no matter of great consequence, but our presence in that place mattered a great deal.

That's what I was thinking about as we made our way in a van toward the Urbana conference.

"Imagine this place," he said.

Ramez Atallah, one of the leaders of the Bible Society of Egypt, stood on the platform during the opening session of the conference, painting a vivid picture of a community of garbage dwellers in Egypt. He urged us to imagine the smell of it, the inescapable hopelessness of it, and then to imagine the young missionary couple who went to this place.

We imagined this couple made the decision to live among these people, in this horrible place, in order to somehow gain their trust, somehow prove their love to them. Then we imagined this couple became pregnant, and they purposed to have their baby in the same manner as the local inhabitants of this place, atop a pile of trash, without anesthesia or modern medicine, as an expression of love for the people of this community.

"Can you imagine this?" he asked us. "If you can, it is because you have never been to this place—this dirty, filthy place, where people live like animals. No self-respecting, middle-class, wealthy couple would ever dare to even conceive of the idea of having their first-born child in that very dangerous place. This has never happened. In all likelihood it never will."

Yet, as Mr. Atallah pointed out, this is exactly what almighty God did. He sent his Son to be born in the filth of a barn, let loose from the safety of heaven, among a broken people, in an attempt to convince them of his unfailing love. God, with reckless abandon, did something that none of us, however committed, could do: He risked.

He became flesh. This is the incarnation.[1]

The thing about Urbana is it's huge.

I'd never been before, and heard only little bits here and there about it, so the largeness of everything took me quite off guard. I'm much more accustomed to missions gatherings being among the least attended events in church. Urbana is like a cross-cultural theme park. Booths too numerous to fully explore in five

1. Atallah, "The Scandal of the Incarnation."

days—from the slick and polished to the more humble variety—are arranged in some categorical manner that requires an advanced degree in urban planning to discern. And the booths are populated with all manner of people, from the hipster twenty-somethings with their smart phones and ironic t-shirts, to the more seasoned field veterans (the old guys) with their maps and ethnic dress. Urbana is so big that it changes the metaphorical landscape of the city, unleashing the potential of thousands of young people on St. Louis for a week. It is a massive and well-oiled machine.

That's one side of the Urbana experience.

The other side is subtler, more inward, like a still, small voice. Urbana is about discerning calling, bringing definition to the quiet whispers inside. If you're open to it, God will use everything from the worship and Bible study to the seminars and the tent city of booths to blow your mind again and again until you're trailing tiny bits of it behind you through the halls of the convention center.

The theme of the '09 conference was the incarnation—the Word became flesh and dwelt among us. Speakers told us the incarnation was not only the message, but also ought to be the model for our ministry—that we should dwell among the people to whom we were called. And they urged us again and again to look for calling at the intersection of our greatest passions and the deepest needs of the world. Of course that statement, while profound, bred some questions. What was I passionate about? And how could I figure out where that passion intersected with a world in need? The answers were supposed to involve Urbana somehow, but they also involved a fast-paced inward journey.

I lifted my hands in worship, took notes during the sessions, wept at some of the stories, and made my way through the booths that seemed like they might have something to do with me. I fed my body with caffeine and my spirit with tired prayers, and I tried my best to listen. While my wife stayed home fielding calls from our parents as to whether or not we had yet made the decision to steal their granddaughter and ruin the remainder of their lives, I had the task of drinking from the fire hose of Urbana and trying to come away with some clarity.

This was the next stage of our calling: definition, specificity.

I spent most of the time just feeling overwhelmed.

"So many of us prize the speed at which we can achieve results, but God's way was slow, subversive, quiet. His was the incarnational way. And Jesus tells us, 'As the Father sent me, so I send you.'"[2]

Oscar Muriu, a pastor from Nairobi, spoke to the Urbana auditorium about what incarnational ministry should look like. He said we must have an attitudinal relocation from a place of pride to a place of humility. We must move from a place of power to a place of vulnerability, so that we will depend less on ourselves and count on the kingdom. We should move from a place of privilege to a place of poverty, such that we must rely on the local communities in which we dwell. And as we move from a place of harmony and unity into a place of chaos and brokenness, we will eventually belong to the community. Just like Jesus, we must belong before we can reform.

Humility. Vulnerability. Poverty. Chaos and brokenness. More prophetic words have rarely been spoken over my life.

By day three I was maxing out the exhaustion gauge.

I went to a Chinese restaurant for lunch and my fortune cookie read, "You are sensitive to all that is going on around you."

I didn't feel sensitive. I felt tired—tired and inundated. I was spending every un-programmed moment trying to process my calling—my deepest passions, and how they intersected with needs in the world. But my mind stood on the verge of spiraling out of control. I tried to go the prayer room and sort through all the ideas cascading around my brain, but the quiet atmosphere and contemplative music almost put me to sleep.

Wading through all the possibilities vying for my life was no small challenge.

2. Muriu, Urbana '09.

The seminars were extremely helpful in that they helped me to discern what I was (and what I was not) passionate about. To begin with, I circled all the seminars that appeared to make sense for me on paper—talks that sounded like maybe God had been shaping me for this thing or that thing. But I attended a seminar involving my vocation and didn't feel stirred by it in the least. It just made me tired.

Other seminars, talks I attended that might not have made as much vocational sense, spoke to the deep longings of my soul. For example, I attended a seminar entitled, "Birthing Missional Communities on the Field," led by members of several different organizations.

I've never been great at community. I recognize a deep-set American value of individualism that roars within me whenever I'm forced to depend on others. I'm not saying that's a good thing; I'm just saying it's there.

On paper, a seminar on community should have felt like a root canal, but it didn't. "We weren't put on this planet to live as safely as possible and then die," Nigel Paul said. "We're supposed to find those on this planet who are not safe, and join them."[3]

I was run over with the realities of missional communities around the world. My heart soared throughout the seminar, evidence to me that the inklings I felt inside—that my family and I needed to be mobilized by a group that placed a high value on community—were true. This was the counsel of the most high; this was how he led me through Urbana.

But all of that heart soaring and spiraling and processing was threatening to crash my whole system. Engine failure seemed imminent. Eventually the coffee would run out.

To compensate I took a lot of walks. It was cold, and I came to St. Louis from a much warmer place. I didn't know how to walk on icy sidewalks without slipping, but I needed time away from the missional sprawl, time to quiet my soul and listen. So I walked.

3. Paul, Urbana '09.

I remember one walk being longer than most. I'd just listened to a lecture on the discipleship of an artist—absolutely one of the best lectures I've ever heard in my life. I spent about an hour walking the city trying to process the lecture until I finally decided to track down the speaker and ask him as Andrew asked Jesus, "Rabbi, where are you staying?"[4] He might not have gotten the joke, and now that I think about it I might not have intended it as a joke, but I purposed to find him and at least let him know how much his talk had meant to me.

I'd heard someone say the speaker might be hanging out in the lounge of a particular hotel, and I searched, but by the time I found the lounge, my future Rabbi's trail had gone cold.

I wanted to tell him that his words had quickened my heart, that they were still resonating inside my chest, that they had helped catalyze something inside me, even though I didn't know exactly what it was yet.

Intense moments of revelation often shock the body, such that one's senses are heightened for a lingering period—warm breath on the lips, or a tolling bell in the distance—like an iris recalibrating when the lights come back on. I think our bodies grope for the meaning that just flashed by, trying to catch its trail again, or at least revel in its fragrance. And so much of the Urbana experience is like this.

My walk through the city that night was just an effort to follow the trail of that fragrance of revelation. I paid attention to my shadows on that walk. I made effort to notice the things that lined up on that walk. I was moving toward a place of clarity.

I already had more in my journal and on my heart than I could process, so I skipped the final New Year's Eve session and went back to the hotel. I made a long list of pros and cons and organizations I'd touched base with at various booths. I read over my notes from the sessions and reflected on words from various speakers: York Moore, who cited examples of atrocities all over the world and said, "We do not need to be persuaded long of the existence of absolute evil."[5]

4. John 1:38b ESV.
5. Moore, "Vision of Another World.

John Franklin, who said, "We must be full of grace and truth. We must tell the truth with everything we make, and everything we do."[6] Patrick Fung, who urged us, "Live to be forgotten."[7]

What was I most passionate about?

How did those passions intersect with the needs of the world?

I confess that I had a lot of exciting ideas that never panned out. But I also had a deep conviction, a profound notion of purpose.

That night, I wrote these words in my journal:

How can I keep secret the most beautiful thing I believe? As I reflect on it, I don't long to share it. But I believe that I can share it, and I believe that I must.

I didn't have one particular country or organization in mind, but by the end of the night I had a few definite routes to pursue, all in the same region of the world. I had friends for whom I intended to pray and neighbors with whom I intended to share the gospel. I had organizations and contacts from Urbana with whom to follow up, and some long-term options to pray over. Our calling had begun to take on definition.

I filled out a decision card: "I want to commit the next season of my life to those who don't know Jesus."

6. Franklin, "Building the Artist: A Spiritual Foundation."
7. Fung, Urbana '09.

four

Opposition

I OPENED MY EYES wide at 5:00 a.m., a month after the Urbana conference, instantly awake. This being atypical for me, I tried to discern what it was that had woken me, but the house was quiet. I thought backward into my dreams, and it seemed like I had been composing a support letter in my head while I was sleeping. Something about it felt very sharp, and I wondered if perhaps God had woken me up for a reason.

Since I was awake anyway, and since it was strange, I decided to get out of bed and pray.

I prayed for my wife, who had been understandably stressed—our future in the air as it was—and I prayed for my daughter. I prayed for my mother- and father-in-law, and for my parents as well, to come to terms with our decision to go. I sought God in the morning, and I sensed the closeness of his Spirit, and I cried a little.

The tears in my eyes burned furiously, and I rushed to the sink to wash them out. I remembered something in Acts about scales on someone's eyes, but I couldn't recall the context, so I looked it up. I wondered, was I Saul, in need of sight, or was I Ananias, awakened to pray for an enemy?[1]

Or should I just stop wearing my contacts to bed?

1. Acts 9:17–18.

I prayed for clarity and direction, a prayer oft upon my lips those days. In that moment God reminded me of how he'd spoken before, how he'd made me certain of things, like the decision to get married, and how he'd orchestrated the big events of my life so precisely that I could not deny his hand. I felt him whisper that he would do the same this time, that I would know when it was right.

I was amazed, as I often am, by the beauty of God, and his love for us.

I couldn't sleep after that. The day went on as usual on the outside, but inside I felt peculiar. I was certain of something without knowing what the something was. It was strange, and beautiful.

A week later we had a Skype interview with the organization through which we would eventually be mobilized. The interview lasted about two hours, and by the end my wife and I were equally full of two sentiments: excitement, and doubt.

We had expected the excitement. It had been building in us for months. But we were very surprised by the doubt. Things we never worried about before sprung up almost instantly: our daughter's health, financial responsibility, being foreigners. We concluded the interview and agreed to come back with an answer for the sending organization in two weeks.

Those were two of the most difficult weeks of our lives.

The third stage of our calling—the commitment to a sending agency—was more specific than the previous two stages, and also more spiritually demanding. I suppose we should have expected opposition. We knew well enough to know that we have an enemy, and that he gets particularly agitated when we incline our ears to great dreams from God. But we had become so intent upon discerning God's voice that we forgot about the other voice—the voice with different words and a different tone, but just as capable of stirring us at the core of our being.

As soon as the interview was over, as soon as the prospect of moving to a specific location became real, we were flooded with misgivings. Our sending organization seemed pretty good. They listed community and discipleship as core values, and they were all about evangelism, so we assumed we would be pushed in the areas we knew we needed to grow. We would live among the people to whom we desired to minister, and the organization took its leadership from the local church. These were all the things God had suggested to us as priorities, and this organization prized them. On the other hand, we'd just met them. "We don't even know these people," we said to ourselves. "Just because they say they value community doesn't guarantee we'll be cared for." How could we really trust them?

The answer, of course, was that if God was calling us, then our trust was secure. But we weren't convinced of that yet. Becoming convinced was the business of stage three.

It was unusual for us to worry about things like that. God had never failed us before; what reason did we have to doubt? Yet the doubts came like waves against the fragile beach of our calling.

Was it financially responsible to leave a job during a down economy and go on partial support? Our parents didn't think so. Was it wise to take a two-year-old prone to fevers to a country where we couldn't speak the language, couldn't communicate with a doctor, couldn't buy medicine?

As we waded the unfamiliar waters of worry, the enemy also cried out our sins. I thought about how judgmental I'd become, at times so full of a spirit of criticism that I ignored the plank in my own eye. I pondered my idol of entertainment. I recognized within myself a deep need for the approval of man—unstable ground, to say the least—and I suddenly felt very frail. Was I a good father? Was I a good husband? Or was I just a selfish child?

As these troubles surfaced they seemed to question the validity of our calling, and the enemy whispered in our ears. *You? Really? God wouldn't call you. Look at yourselves.*

We did look at ourselves. And we doubted our calling.

In addition, things weren't proceeding as well as we would've liked with our commitment to be incarnational with our neighbors.

We'd had them over for a meal, we'd brought them some food on a few other occasions, but we found very little common ground. Our goal was to work up the relationship and the boldness to invite them to a Bible study in our home. The relationship wasn't happening, and neither was the boldness. *If you can't do it here*, the enemy posed, *What makes you think you can do it there?*

We did make one good decision during those two weeks, which was to recognize that we were in a battle and ask discerning friends for prayer and counsel. We were strengthened by their prayers, and encouraged by their words.

One friend prayed Psalm 142 for us, reminding us that even when we are overwhelmed, the Lord is our refuge and portion, and he hears our cries.[2]

My friend Mike had been a missionary and raised a family overseas, and I asked him about going on support. He took me out for coffee and said, "Sometimes you get what you need off the tree, and sometimes the tree is barren and you do without, but you make it. It's better to walk on water and get wet than to stay in the boat, because walking on water is awesome. People might say, 'You shouldn't do that,' in the natural, but we don't live in the natural."

I asked him about our parents' lack of encouragement regarding the decision, and his advice was that parents eventually become proud to partner with you in the King's work.

Probably the best advice we got was from my friend Bernie, a local pastor. "God often allows us to go through a time when our calling is solidified," he said. "It's not fun, but it's what we look back on when the road is hard. It's how we can rest, and know that our calling is sure."

He also pointed out that the enemy was obviously not happy about what we were pursuing, and was aggressively oppressing us in order to scare us away, or distract us from the call.

Surely we sensed a calling. Were it not so, the enemy would not have been so active. We pondered our lives and concluded like

2. Ps 142:5.

many that we are given one turn on this earth, one breath with which to glorify God. How could we look up at him and say, "No?"

This sentiment rose up to drive us: We must serve this God, this King. If what he has done compels us, if we love him, we will follow wherever he leads.

During this period in which our calling was made sure, we discovered this principle to be quite easy as a principle, and much harder as a practice. I sent an email to the director of our sending organization and let him know the kinds of things we were processing. His answer was brief, but insightful.

"There are only two questions that matter right now," he said. "Is God calling you to this country? And is he calling you to go with us? All your other questions will work themselves out over time."

That felt right.

We felt compelled to go, and drawn to stay, but we began to perceive it as the Spirit urging us to go, and the flesh begging us to stay. And if that was true, our answer was pretty cut and dry.

At last, God spoke. We asked him for assurance about our daughter's health and the next day she became sick with a very high fever. We threw up our hands and said, "See! This is what we were worried about!"

We took her to a doctor who said something like, "Well, you know, give her fluids and Tylenol."

We got home and my wife and I both felt God whisper to us, "What's the difference? You have fluids and Tylenol here, and you have it there. Who really guards your daughter's life?"

We were humbled. In fact, God had been speaking the same thing to us throughout our two weeks of worries and temptations and doubts and counsel. He had been speaking even through the trials themselves. Like the resolving chord of a song, like a steadfast, immoveable foundation, he spoke, "I am faithful, and I am enough."

Was it wise to leave a salary position and go on support? "I am faithful, and I am enough."

Would we survive so far from our friends and family? "I am faithful, and I am enough."

Could we trust the sending agency to which we had applied? "I am faithful, and I am enough."

Nothing the enemy could say was any match for this.

And this became true of every single one of our doubts as we laid them before the Lord. We looked to God, and he gently answered all of our uncertainty with the same words. He met our misgivings with the surety of his presence. He answered all of our fears with himself, and in so doing he made our calling sure.

After the two weeks we made a verbal commitment to go.

five

Walking Through a Door

One of my favorite poets of all time is Li-Young Lee. He's a Chinese American Pulitzer Prize winner who writes beautifully spacious words about family, and memory, and love. Some lines from his poem, "This Room and Everything in It," go like this:

> Lie still now
> while I prepare for my future,
> certain hard days ahead,
> when I'll need what I know so clearly this moment.
> I am making use
> of the one thing I learned
> of all the things my father tried to teach me:
> the art of memory.
>
> I am letting this room
> and everything in it
> stand for my ideas about love
> and its difficulties.[1]

The poem goes on to describe things in the room, and how he finds himself in those things and understands something of what love is like in that moment, and then purposes to recall those moments at a later time.

---

1. Lee, *The City in Which I Love You*, 49.

Edge of the Map

Lee's poem continues:

and so on, each thing
standing for a separate idea,
and those ideas forming the constellation
of my greater idea.
And one day, when I need
to tell myself something intelligent
about love,

I'll close my eyes
and recall this room and everything in it.[2]

As my wife, my daughter and I set out for our new home in the summer of 2010, these lines were heavy on my mind. We brought eight checked bags, filled exactly to the weight limit, six carry-on bags, one car seat (which we would never use again) and a stroller. We were quite the caravan.

Entering a new stage of life is like walking through a door—or, in our case, stumbling through a door with two hundred pounds on your shoulders, trying not to drop the baby.

We stepped off the third airplane, collected our bags, and found our director waiting for us with a smile—which trembled slightly at its edges upon seeing our mountains of luggage. My daughter had slept peacefully through most of the travel and was wide awake; my wife and I were not. We were ready to collapse into the taxi, but we had too many bags for one, or even two taxis to manage. We took three separate taxis—myself in one, my wife and daughter in the other, and our director in the third—stuffed them with our belongings, and arrived at our hotel at 11:00 p.m. local time.

I tossed a suitcase onto one of the beds and a cloud of dust flew up from the bedspread as though I'd just opened a sarcophagus. We turned on the shower and the smell of rotten eggs filled our room. We looked at each other, gritted our teeth, and nodded. There was no turning back now.

2. Lee, *The City in Which I Love You*, 50.

I like the way Peterson translates Proverbs 11:5 in *The Message*: "Moral character makes for smooth traveling; an evil life is a hard life."[3]

Even in those first difficult weeks I believed these words—an evil life would have been harder. Then again, I probably wouldn't have described our transition as entirely smooth.

"This Room and Everything in It" spoke to me about our transition. The "room" was our period of calling, and the things I clung to were experiences, words from God, and the personal realizations made during those various stages of calling. We had told God we were willing to go. We had sought definition and specificity. We had faced opposition and come through it trusting God even more on the other side. Those were important things, foundational things, and I had written them on my heart.

But if I told you I was absolutely certain of our call as I stepped onto that airplane, it would be a lie.

It had taken us about a year to move from that first "yes" to touching down in a new country, but for all God had done during that year, all the clarity and assurance he'd given us, all the faithfulness he'd shown, a part of me still doubted.

We spent our final three months in America raising support and saying goodbyes. We traveled to churches and homes of friends, held up our daughter like the opening scene of the Lion King and waited for people to take out their wallets, and bid farewell to familiarity for at least two years (the length of our initial commitment).

We came to gauge the level of trust a church had in us by the venue they bestowed upon us. Some churches kept us at a distance—some space on a table in the foyer, or one among many booths in the lobby. Other churches invited us to make an announcement or give a testimony for between-five-and-absolutely-no-longer-than-seven

3. Prov 11:5 The Message.

minutes. Still others invited us to join the worship team, or to lead a song. They gave us the entire service to preach and describe what we'd be doing overseas and they prayed over us as a congregation.

We trusted God to bring in enough support, and he did, of course, but we were surprised, as is often the case, by who gave to us financially and who did not. Some friends committed to donate monthly support even though they couldn't find full-time work. Some even made radical commitments, like canceling their lawn services, committing to maintain their yards themselves in order to have enough money to help us get overseas. Others politely navigated around the question of financial support, if they acknowledged it at all.

Some of our friends and family went out of their way to see us before we left; others didn't even make the time to drive a few blocks. People we considered close friends surprised us by not making time to say goodbye, and this affected us more than we'd expected. It was a strange time for us, socially.

News from the field shifted on a weekly basis during those three months. The site where we originally planned to go was no longer an option. We went several weeks without a destination or an employer in-country, which meant we couldn't get visas. Then, once a location was settled upon, we learned we would no longer be with our originally planned site team. We would be the only married couple at our site, and the only family with a child.

God has the habit of rearranging our plans to suit his purposes.

We knew his goodness very well, but that didn't stop us from questioning him and our field director. Wasn't community supposed to be a core value? How were we supposed to figure out how to raise a child overseas when we were the only family at our site? Every email we got from the field seemed to further complicate our plans.

Then there was the "how do you get a two-year-old a visa" fiasco, and the health insurance debacle, and a dozen other logistical issues for which we had no plan. Our field director was some help, but with parents who still hadn't grown comfortable with the idea, and friends who were busy enough managing their own lives, we spent several months wading through our anxieties alone.

This final stage of our calling was the transition period—the brief space between lives. Yes, God had told us his grace was sufficient. And it was a good thing he did, because if he hadn't we would have given up before we even got out of the country.

Shutting down an entire life in one place and starting up a life in another place was a whole lot of work. Some doors closed nicely behind us as we made our exit and others squealed like they hadn't been greased in a decade.

Our home church, where we had served for more than five years, held a service for us full of many tears. People stood behind us financially and prayerfully. We had been worried that no one would step up to lead the ministries we had helmed, but God, in his sovereignty, provided the perfect people to come in behind us. We felt very cherished by our church family, honored to be sent by them, and also released by them to go.

Other areas of our lives did not give us such a warm, fuzzy feeling. As we left the country, many of our friends were in the midst of difficult spiritual battles. Couples facing divorce, bitterness between family members, and a lack of communication from many of our close friends weighed heavily upon our hearts.

Though the door of my office at work had seemed to shut smoothly, I learned that my boss's boss's boss did not intend to re-hire my position since the institution, like the rest of the economy, was financially strapped. I worried about what would become of the program I'd helped to shepherd for six years of my life.

And there were a thousand little things—cell phone contracts, email addresses, immunizations, bills. I had naively hoped that our transition period would be a centering time of anticipation. We had good moments, but most of our days languished away in frustration and triviality. And one anxious thought was chief among the rest of our anxieties: What were we going to do with our two-year-old?

We didn't know what our ministry was going to look like. We didn't know what transportation in-country would look like. We didn't know what she could eat, or where she would sleep, or if she would have any friends, or how to say she was allergic to milk and eggs in the local language. What would we do with her for a three-day orientation? She was too shy to just run off with a new babysitter who couldn't speak English. As a father I was deeply concerned, worried even, about how she would manage the transition.

Even as we stepped onto the plane I wondered if what we were doing was best for our little girl.

Later we would learn how to manage the dust problem. We would find that the rotten egg smell was only occasional, and we would have many people to help us along the way. But for that first night, one of us taking a shift to play with our well-rested daughter through the wee hours while the other one tossed in a filthy bed, we cast ourselves before the Lord with one painful and tired question: Why? Why did you call us here? Can't you see we're not cut out for it? Don't you know us well enough to know that we don't know how to live here, much less how to serve you here?

Like Li Young Lee's poem, I thought back to the memories of the previous six months in an effort to remember something important.

I thought of that map in the foyer of my father's church and wondered if perhaps they had left this location off because they simply couldn't fathom it. Certainly I hadn't been able to conceive of it before my arrival, and now that I had arrived, I felt very much off the radar of my community back home, out of sight and out of mind—off the edge of the map.

I remembered our former ministries—their sweetness as well as their bitterness—and I wondered if discontentment might be preferable to lying in that bed. I remembered my struggles with idolatry, and I wondered if apathy might not be preferable to smelling like sulfur. I remembered the strong words from the speakers at Urbana and I wondered if I had somehow missed the part where they talked about feeling lost and alone. I remembered the voice of opposition, the jester-like voice of the enemy, stifling a laugh as he whispered my faults to me again and again—isolationism, a judgmental attitude, displaced identity, a lack of reliance upon the Lord.

I tossed and turned, all those ideas forming the constellation of my greater idea, which was supposed to be something about the nature of calling, and my reason for following God off the edge of the map. But try as I might I couldn't convince myself of the rightness of our decision.

Then, like a smash cut in a movie, I was suddenly awake. It was 5:00 a.m. My daughter was asleep in the middle of my bed and there was no room for me to lie down. Since I was awake anyway, and since it was strange, I got up and tried to pray.

I sat on the edge of my bed, looking down at my sleeping girl, and I sensed the Holy Spirit draw near. Before I could even ask him to turn all my complaints to praise, he did, and I wept at his grace, at the beauty of it. All of my tiny sufferings were privileges, occasions for joy. And this was it; this was serving God. My spirit soared at this thought.

I prayed for my family, for my friends back home—the ones who had made time for me and the ones who hadn't—and for the teammates I had yet to meet. When I stopped praying and opened my heart to listen, God spoke a word to me that sent a tremor through my being.

For two years, since my daughter had been born, I had asked the Lord to teach me how to give her a godly heritage, a spiritual inheritance rather than a financial one. In that moment I sat speechless as God told me that he would do this. Since we had surrendered our girl, offered her up by bringing her here in obedience to his call, he would give her a spiritual foundation. An anointing. He would bless her.

I was so sure of his voice in that moment, like I have been only a few times in my life. And I was so very, very grateful. God confirmed to me in the person of my daughter that I had made the right decision. I looked down at her, and I believed what God said, and I knew.

Even now, this is what I look back on—his favor in that moment—as his seal upon our calling.

We had a long way to go. Our journey off the map had only just begun, but it began with a word of his favor. No matter how difficult things would get in the days to come, no matter how many disappointments we would face or tears we would shed, we would not be able to deny this truth: God had called us to this place, for this time. Of that there was no longer any room for doubt.

PART TWO

Adjustment

six

A Torch in the Fog

THE SMALL ROOM, HUMID with the presence of our team huddled together on the tile felt crowded, but safe, a shelter from the brisk September air, and from the fog outside—a thick cloud of mist mingled with polluted air, shrouding our city in a bitter, white blanket. We knelt together in prayer. We thanked God together, most of us strangers to one another, but bound by mutual blessing, the privilege of serving as ambassadors of the King. We sang songs about him. We asked him for help and he spoke to us. We took refuge in that warm place, together.

As I waited on the Lord in worship, I felt him say to us, "Come as you are." I was grateful to serve a God who knows our frame, remembers that we are made from dust,[1] and invites us in before we're clean. It was particularly relevant to me that morning because I didn't show up to our first team gathering in a very good mood.

For one thing, we had yet to adjust to the time change. We still walked like zombies through the day and slept with our eyes wide open at night. We were stressed, which for my wife meant lots of complaining and for me meant a short fuse—not the best combination. Here we were on the mission field, confident in the promise and calling of God, yet full of protest and quarrel.

1. Ps 103:14.

I wonder if I was so disillusioned as to think that having answered the call we would become instantly holy. It seems ridiculous now, but my actual notions may not have been too far from this at the time.

I had spent so much time closing down my former life and setting up the logistics of my new life that I hadn't taken time to mentally prepare for waking up in a new country. I was there, but I wasn't ready to be there. The white fog outside mirrored the haze in my head, one thought hidden from the next by a thick veil, a mental pall through which I stumbled to that first meeting.

My wife and I arrived certain that one of us would have to sit the gathering out in order to watch our daughter. Our organization had hired some babysitters for the eight kids between us, but we had no illusions of her trusting a new babysitter. Our daughter didn't trust new people; she ran from them. Back home, she never even went to the church nursery unless one of us was present. And back home, the nursery workers could speak her language.

So the word "miracle" is an appropriate description of what happened.

The three of us were sitting on the floor together as worship began. The other children had already left the room, but our daughter had no intention of following them out. One of the babysitters came over and sat down with us. She didn't say anything; she just started building a little block tower with our daughter. After a minute she said, "I'm Deborah. Do you want to come play with me?"

Our daughter stood, held her stuffed animal in one hand, and let Deborah lead her out of the room by the other.

My jaw hit the floor. This had never happened. We would not have deemed it possible. Yet she didn't look back, and she played with Deborah and the other children for the duration of the meeting.

These were the kinds of surprises God had in store for us. Things so small, but so real, built our faith one block at a time. In tiny increments he made a way for us to hear him speak into the cloud.

At that meeting our new team prayed very special prayers over us. They prayed a blessing of going out and coming in—speaking to our period of transition. They prayed we would adapt quickly. They said God was calling me to be a leader. They saw me formerly running down a track, holding a torch with an orange flame; but said I would now run through a forest, holding a torch that burned a much hotter blue. They said my wife was a gifted friend-maker. They said she and our daughter would be beloved by the people of our new nation. They prayed for her to take ownership of her ministry as a mother and evangelist, and for her to submit to God's blessing and plan.

Over the next week of orientation, God continued to present his vision for our team, and what that meant for us personally. He gave us eyes to see through the fog.

The vision statement of our sending agency began with an emphasis on community. Our desire to do ministry alongside others was one of the reasons we settled on the agency in the first place. We knew we needed people around us. We knew we needed help.

On the other hand, I'm American, and the individualism label definitely applies to me. I like to do things for myself. I don't want people around me. I don't want help.

Obviously, I had a problem.

For orientation we met in a team member's apartment. As our leader scribbled the core values of our agency on a white board I looked around the room at the unfamiliar faces with whom I was supposed to learn to do cross-cultural ministry. Everyone seemed nice, of course, glowing with the newness of an un-proven bicycle. Everyone seemed serious about the objective at hand. I felt safe in assuming we all shared a certain level of commitment; after all, we had all left home to follow Jesus.

But that's where the apparent similarities ended. One look at our group photo suggested a very unlikely family. We were all different ages, at different stages in life. We all came from different places. We had different accents, different skin colors, different sets of facial expressions. The more we opened our mouths, the more we began to realize how dissimilar we actually were: different family situations, different denominational backgrounds, different hobbies and strengths and weaknesses and fears and buttons. Our diversity was instantly evident, and we were certain to discover many more of its facets in time.

But God is very good at building families.

In an overseas context you are much more aware of your neediness. You are forced to depend on one another. If you're single, you need companionship; if you have a family, you need help with your kids. Even experienced cross-cultural workers need someone to help them adjust to and engage in life in a new setting. And these needs are good; these needs facilitate unity.

When Jesus prays for us in John 17, he prays, "That they may be one even as we are one, I in them and you in me, that they may become perfectly one, so that the world may know that you sent me and loved them even as you loved me."[2]

The book of Acts describes this oneness with each other at the end of its second chapter (from which many contemporary churches take their names). The chapter speaks of devotion, fellowship, the breaking of bread, and prayer. It says those who believed shared their possessions to meet the needs of the body. It concludes by saying, "And the Lord added to their number day by day those who were being saved."[3]

Both of these Scriptures speak to community, and both of them end with people seeing the truth of God and turning to him.

Simply put: Community leads to evangelism.

Our agency's commitment to evangelism was another reason it surfaced to the top of our decision pool. As previously stated, we didn't consider ourselves particularly gifted evangelists. We wouldn't have numbered it among our strengths, and the prayers our team prayed over us felt challenging to accept.

Still, we are among those who hold to the opinion that there is still a work for Westerners to do on the mission field, and that it doesn't just involve sending money. It can be a convenient excuse

2. John 17:22b–23 ESV.
3. Acts 2:47b NIV.

to suggest that nationals ought to be the only ones engaged in the evangelism of their own people, but that insinuation ignores the power of incarnation. Certainly, there are some contexts in which Westerners can still act as messengers of the gospel, in which they might even enjoy an advantage or two. Certainly we can still reflect the light that casts out darkness.

During orientation we studied the parable of the minas in Luke 19. Each servant was given the same amount, and the master did not ask them to be profitable, but to do business.[4] Perhaps the more successful servant was shrewder with what he had been given; perhaps he was just more fortunate, but he did business.

If the mina is our life—our time on this earth—then we ought to invest it wisely, but we also trust God to provide a return on our investment. Profitability is not our concern.

This took some of the pressure off of our charge to evangelism (though we still looked on it with a degree of trepidation). The other way we made peace with our mission was finding confidence in our relationship with the local church.

Admittedly, there must come a time when a new believer must be discipled by a member of his or her own culture, which is why our agency states its primary function is to serve the local church. We are connected to multiple congregations, and consider ourselves subservient to the local church leadership.

As I sat in the apartment learning these things, I recalled the lessons of Urbana. I didn't know the local language, and I had zero personal connection to the local church, but belonging to an organization that did have these things made me feel safe. It made me feel covered. We were not just single-minded workers from the West intent upon fulfilling our own agenda. We submitted to a local, ecclesiastic authority structure.

Even being an American, I liked that.

4. Luke 19:13.

During orientation, our director asked us two questions: "What baggage did you bring with you? And what do you want to take away after this semester?"

He gave us forty-five minutes to crank out an answer.

I wrote about the traces of judgment I'd been noticing, and the oversensitivity—the need for approval. I also wrote about my war with selfishness, with the desire to be entertained and the flesh that craves comfort.

All these things were true of me, but they were also surface problems. They were symptoms.

At the time, I didn't recognize a lot of the baggage I carried for what it really was. I called it by other names, or blamed it on other things, but the roots of my trouble ran to depths I had yet to explore.

I wrote that I wanted to end the semester with my feet more fully beneath me (as opposed to flailing about in the air as I tumbled head-over-heels through the foreignness of our new home). I wanted to know my way around, know how to order food and shop for basic necessities. I wanted to know my new teammates—how to serve them and how to love them. I wanted to find myself closer to God at the end of the semester than I had been four months prior. I also wanted to more fully understand and embrace the vision of the sending agency I'd joined.

I couldn't have known at that time, that each of these goals would in fact lead me to the discovery of those subterranean roots that fed the host of my personal issues. I didn't know that what I was actually seeking was much, much deeper.

The branches that bear fruit, he prunes, that they will bear more fruit still.[5] But I didn't understand that yet.

"God invited you here because he loves you," our team leader told us.

5. John 15:2b.

We hadn't considered that. We imagined him telling us to go, not inviting us; we felt more like children obediently doing chores than children opening a gift on Christmas morning.

But something about that statement felt so true. God invited us, because he loved us.

Near the end of orientation we received some tough news from home. One of our family members was suddenly ill, very near death. Our friends' marital troubles had deepened. Another of our friends had a miscarriage.

Contrary to what we might have thought, joining God on mission didn't lead us to a charmed life. We were still exhausted and irritable, still unsure of our footing. Our problems didn't go away. In fact, they reared their heads quite violently.

But we had something we didn't have before: a plan.

Joining an agency with a vision for ministry was critical to our survival as individuals and as a family. Community, evangelism, and submission to the local church: chief tenants of our organization that would push us to engage with the culture and disciple us toward personal spiritual growth. Even as I heard it for the first time, I was so grateful for the plan—something to aim for, instead of just groping my way through the fog.

As I stood up from that tile floor and walked from the apartment back to our hotel, carrying my sleeping daughter in my arms, scarcely able to see ten steps in front of me through the quilted white, I wondered what it would be like to carry a blue torch through a forest. What creatures might lurk there, just beyond my vision? How hot might the flame need burn in order to light my steps? Hot enough to keep the cold at bay? Hot enough to purify me?

It felt like we had so much to do. It felt overwhelming and impossible. But we had already seen miracles from God. And now he had given us a vision.

seven

Our New Body

CANVAS SCRAPED AGAINST CONCRETE, one step at a time. The strength to lift our final duffle bag escaped me, so I bent at the waist, heaving the mammoth beast in both hands as I squat-walked up the staircase backwards. Muscles I never used filed their complaints. The duffle bag seemed to stretch into a comically long version of itself as I tugged. The guy at Army/Navy had assured me this duffle, while cheap, was incredibly sturdy. I prayed he was right as sweat dripped from my face, trickled down my arms, and soaked into the bag.

Scrape, thump!

Scrape, thump!

Scrape, thump!

The sound of the bag sliding up and coming to rest on each step bled monotonously into my ears and I wondered if I might pass out.

"I'll be fine," I thought. "As long as it doesn't—"

RIP!

The seam in the bag could finally take no more. The canvas burst and the possessions we'd hauled across an ocean exploded in the staircase. I fell back on the steps and my nerve endings burned as I took in the crime scene: books, toys, and clothes scattered chaotically amidst the grime and moisture of the dank steps, and the dust cloud risen from the explosion settling in the air.

"This is my life now," I said.

My muscles seized again as I crept back down the stairs like a downcast soldier, gathering my daughter's books like fallen comrades. The whole thing was very dramatic.

We'd been in country for more than three weeks, but we had yet to set foot in our apartment. The supervisor at our school (where we would be employed) said they were still preparing our permanent residence, so we and our fourteen bags, car seat and stroller, bounced from hotel to hotel throughout the city, waiting. Every trip took multiple taxis, and the hotel rooms barely had enough floor space to accommodate what we began to consider a ridiculous amount of luggage. We were quite the traveling spectacle.

When move-in day finally came, exhaustion from all the caravanning had taken its toll. We just wanted a place to sit down and unpack. Cranky and sore, we heaved our split-seamed luggage up the eighty-two steps—one of our eight duffle bags perishing in the flight—only to find that "preparing" our apartment had not entailed cleaning our apartment.

The place was filthy.

The few appliances we'd inherited were yellowed and only about half of them worked. Fragrant brown water flowed from the tap. Paint flecks from moldy cracks in the ceiling drifted down like snow, and a sticky film of dust blanketed every centimeter of the floor. One of the rooms was padlocked shut, hiding things we couldn't imagine to be worse than what was out in the open.

We made footprints in the dust, placing our weathered bags in different rooms, trying not to ring our crestfallen hands with too great a noise. Eventually we just sat down on the sagging couch and stared at the off-white walls. Where to begin?

Then there was a knock at the door.

One by one, our teammates came up from their own apartments on the floor below us. Their rooms had been newly furnished and renovated, but were not large enough to accommodate a family. Thus, we had been granted a den of dust with the mysterious padlocked room.

Our new friends looked around the large space and set about finding buckets and soap. They bought a few mops from the store downstairs. They used some old t-shirts as rags. They beat our couch cushions and scrubbed our toilets and scoured the inside of the refrigerator and helped us make lists of things to buy. In less than two hours, the place was clean.

Eventually the water would flow clear, if not drinkable. We would learn how to keep the dust at bay. Our contact at the school would bring us a "special tool" to open the padlock on the third bedroom (it was a hammer), and we would get some new shelves and kitchen fixtures. Eventually it would be home.

But on that first day, when our new teammates cleaned our apartment with us, we realized with a pang of contented clarity that our "home" was not made of walls and furniture and crumbling paint, but of a body, of a fellowship, of people.

School had yet to begin, so our site team took advantage of its honeymoon stage to draw close together. A certain level of vulnerability came easily as we had yet to find reasons to withhold trust. Even on a honeymoon, there's nothing instant about intimacy, so we made great effort to redeem our time together.

Each member of our site team led an evening prayer time, which was a great way to get to know one another. One team member led us in the confession of sins, another in a focus on the portraits of God in Scripture. One led a time of reflection on the cross, and another led a slow reflection on Isaiah 30: "In repentance and rest is your salvation; in quietness and trust is your strength."[1] Evening by evening we learned what different teammates valued, how they approached the gospel and their relationship with God, how they struggled and where they were strong. Naive though we may have been to the oncoming frustrations and disunity we would face together, those early prayer times laid a solid foundation for real intimacy.

We spent a lot of time with each other in those first weeks. We explored the city, trying new foods and experiencing the culture. Ours was the first full-time team on that particular campus, so we

1. Is 30:15b NIV.

learned together how to find the people and places we needed to find. We had long conversations about past experience and theology. Camaraderie formed around common interests. We shared testimonies and sought out ways to serve one another.

If the cooperative meeting of needs built community, then our family offered a prime opportunity to the site team, because we were extremely needy. A young daughter with food allergies, 0.01 percent fluency in the local language, a droning hum of exhaustion: our needs were immediately apparent to everyone, even before we set foot on campus. This was one of the many ways we hadn't expected God to work through our family. He fostered unity in the team through our neediness.

The needs of the unmarried team members were harder to discern. After team meetings, each of them went back to a lonely apartment, and each of them dealt with that in different ways. One man's blessing was another man's pain in the neck. It took some effort on everyone's part to learn the most appropriate ways to serve and encourage others on the team.

It's worth mentioning here that encouragement is not something that comes naturally to me. I need it desperately, but I give it sparingly. I'm less likely to offer a stumbling friend a hand and more likely to offer him a kick in the pants.

My deficiency in this regard is never more apparent than when my wife gets sick. All she wants is for someone to commiserate with her, to put a cold cloth on her head and tell her everything will be fine. I try, with sincerity, to do this. But I am a horrible nurse. What usually comes out sounds less like encouragement and more like, "Why don't you just suck it up?"

So, on one hand, here I was the recipient of more help than I was comfortable receiving, (remember, I'm an American), and on the other hand I was meant to explore ways of offering help to others that I was—on a nearly genetic level—incapable of offering.

Community, to me, was a challenge.

We had weekly reading assignments and several meetings throughout the week to discuss and process what we were learning. In addition to personal processing, these assignments were meant to facilitate an environment that would build community. We had the team over to our apartment for meals and times of worship, and we went out together on a regular basis. We were all essentially next-door neighbors.

But as we soon found, proximity did not equal intimacy.

Our rough edges emerged when tiredness set up camp in our lives. Politeness was offered with great difficulty to a team member who, say, didn't like to bathe, as he sat on your couch, complaining about the consistency of the omelet you'd just prepared for him, heedless of the fact that your daughter had kept you up through much of the night.

We started rubbing each other the wrong way.

Everyone had different mechanisms to process fatigue. Some attempted to plot a private course of internal suffering, but even the most elaborately concealed frustration was apparent with one living on top of the other. Facial expressions and body language went off like firecrackers.

Others processed everything openly. They wore emotions like lipstick and eyeliner. Small things were monumental things. Tardiness became a huge slap in the face. A stray word could ruin an evening.

The problem with these types of behaviors was the connectedness our proximity allowed. Everything affected everything. One wrong look held the power to bring down the whole ship. Our great mistake in those days was failing to address the problems. All of our efforts toward intimacy had not constructed avenues to deal with community problems, so our team eventually hovered around a slow boil of frustration.

We tried to serve each other, but even that often drove us further from unity. A teammate washed our dishes, for example, but in the process flushed all of our daughter's sippy-cup fixtures down the toilet. Another teammate would bring some food to our place, but it was often a local dish that only he found appetizing, and if we didn't eat it, his feelings might be hurt.

Some people wanted to see more of each other, and some wanted less time together. Some wanted to hear podcast sermons from particular preachers and some wanted different songs—and this was a community of seven people!

Great care must be taken in the building of communities. It does not just happen on its own. But we didn't know that yet.

As far as we knew, there was no expression of church for foreigners in our part of the city, so we spent Sunday mornings together as a site team. We shared a meal, sang some songs, and each team member would take a turn leading time in the Word.

We listened to a sermon on community by Tim Keller during one of our first Sunday gatherings, which offered some important insights for our immediate circumstances.

Keller points out the distinct parallel between the giving of the law through Moses and Christ's famous "sermon on the mount." Like Moses, who went up to the mountain, met with God, and came down with the law, Jesus climbed a mountain with his followers, chose the twelve, then sat down on the mountainside and delivered his sermon. The purpose of the law was to make the Israelites into a nation—a people. The sermon on the mount can likewise be read as a treatise on community. Here is what makes you a people: recognizing the blessedness, the deep satisfaction with life that is not hindered, but is in fact made stronger by things like sacrifice, weakness, grief, and exclusion.[2]

The body of Christ is meant to be a community of radical freedom, wherein we prize what the world calls pitiable, and hold suspect what the world calls great. It's only together that we discover or attain this.[3]

In the context of our new body, we started to see how an unhealthy expression of community could drive us toward things like suffering and weakness and exclusion, while a healthy practice of community could offer respite from the very same things.

2. Keller, "The Community of Jesus."
3. Ibid.

We had an idea of what to aim for, but for a new site team of people who weren't accustomed to radical expressions of community, the bar was set very high.

I walked to a park near our school early one morning, after a particularly difficult time in community the night before. Another foggy day.

I was frustrated with one of my more emotive teammates, and confused as to whether or not I had offended him. I was full of conflicting emotions, only a step or two away from exploding like the duffle bag. I needed a break.

In a small gazebo, set out over a still pond, I sat on a cool, stone bench and watched the water bugs glance across the glass. I could almost see the outlines of their trails through the mist. Scant ripples disturbed the surface at each hectic flutter, and I thought of my new community. No matter how gingerly we danced around each other, the collective stir of our feet upon the earth was still enough to make trouble.

Light from the newly risen sun broke the fog and cast gentle shadows against the pond—the tiled roof, the dancing bugs—intensifying the gleam of the ripples in the water; everything more severe in the light.

In a corner made by two shadows I noticed the water more consistently stirred, as though a silent fountain of steady drops pummeled the surface. I searched, but could not find the source of the stream, only its effect.

Suddenly I longed to be filled with the Spirit.

Not a single drop, but a continual filling, leading to continual ripples. Not a single note, but a symphony, cacophonous stirrings beautifully orchestrated to envelop everything beneath its rippling effect.

This, I knew, was the potential of serving and living in community. If we could yield to the Spirit, if we could harness the promptings of love, our impact upon each other and upon our city would be severe, like the light.

Why was the early church so often exhorted to love one another? Why did Jesus spend so much time talking about it? Why did Paul feel the need to constantly remind Christ's followers to love?

If you've ever lived in a close proximity Christian community then you absolutely know the answer to this question: It's because we're not very good at it.

The body of Christ has always been a diverse group of people. We don't naturally gravitate toward one another, but the commonality we share—our collective adoption—is the most powerful of bonds. Yet it is also paradoxically fragile. When we fail to love, our family can so easily be pulled apart.

Theoretically, no one has a problem with this. Working it out practically is a different story entirely.

While our present context and proximity offered a number of obstacles to community, it should be noted that we also had an advantage: We were breaking the law together.

In our country, we were permitted to believe whatever we wanted to believe, but sharing the truth that had changed our lives and made us a family was illegal. And since a truth like this cannot be kept a secret, our community was somewhat at odds with the letter of the law. This provided numerous occasions for stress, but more than that, it bound us together. We pressed into one another. We annoyed each other and we blessed each other. It was complicated, but we were in it together. As a body, we pressed our shoulders close, and purposed hesitant, sometimes jarring steps down a path still thickly veiled in fog.

As the days went by we began to understand that a deep expression of Christian community meant more than just tolerating differences. It meant somehow moving beyond them. It meant conflict.

eight

Successes, and Failures
. . . Mostly Failures

Today is a bit slower than yesterday, I think. I beat the cushions, finished an update home, folded dry clothes and hung wet clothes up to dry (which, it turns out, takes a lot longer than using a dryer), finished an expense report, organized some dishes, bought some vegetables and did some preparatory reading.

When I will have time to build relationships and spend time with nationals is still a mystery.

When can I make time for that? It's not like I'm just relaxing. Back home I could cut out some kind of leisure in order to make space for people; here I must trim from what I deem necessity.

Mud-caked gravel flew in every direction as I stomped through the neighborhood behind our campus after a mid-morning rain shower. A plastic bag of soup—which I had not (intentionally) ordered—swayed back and forth in my right hand and my daughter clung to my left side as we made our way home after yet another unsuccessful venture in lunchtime.

As a generally healthy two-year-old my daughter could walk, run and jump, and she did all of these with frequency . . . as long as we stayed indoors. Our problem was that the locals in our new country had the unfortunate habit of grabbing children. Where we lived, it was not uncommon for a woman we'd never met to see us from across the street, run toward us in a rapid shower of the local dialect, and whisk our daughter up into her arms. The first time it happened we thought she was being kidnapped. We got used to it soon enough, but it continued to horrify our already timid daughter. For the first three or four months we lived overseas, if we were outside, she insisted on being carried.

When we decided to raise our child in an environment foreign to both of her parents, we knew there would be challenges, but the degree of those challenges still surprised us.

We stood on the playground (which was itself, for all intents and purposes, a public toilet for the neighborhood children) and watched as stranger after stranger would stroke our daughter's blonde hair, press close to her light skin, comment on her beauty and the color of her eyes. Not that it wasn't flattering, but being perpetually singled-out takes a toll on a child. On our family excursion to the local zoo, the patrons turned from the animal exhibits and began snapping pictures of our sullen daughter as she tried to hide her face in the stroller like a haggard celebrity.

But the worst was the clothes.

No matter how many layers, no matter how thick the fabric, a walk outdoors in the crisp, autumn air would elicit a minimum of five rebukes, without fail.

"Her clothes are too thin!"

"She's not wearing enough clothes!"

"You really shouldn't have her out in this weather at all."

"Don't they know how to dress where you're from?"

"More clothes!"

Every. Single. Time.

Of course, this chiding took place in the local language, of which we spoke hardly a word, but our friendly advisors found ways to make themselves understood. They pinched her jacket, tugged at her pants, scowled and shook their heads in disapproval.

On this particular day I had set out with great confidence. I had practiced the pronunciation of my favorite dish until proficient. I had quickly found the stall that carried said dish. I had quite confidently ordered what I wanted. I had failed.

I tried several more times, eventually settling on a dish I didn't even want as the vendor pointed out my daughter's ankle peeking from between a double layer of socks and the leg of her sweatpants.

Communication failures came with such frequency in those days that we didn't even try to keep track. Yet we found ourselves unconsciously measuring our success on the field with our success (or lack thereof) in cultural forays.

I tried to order a bus ticket, for example, repeating my desired stop over and over in carefully practiced intonation, only to be met by an irritated expression in the ticket taker's eye. Sooner or later another passenger would understand what I wanted, pronounce my stop for me in what was (to my ears) exactly the same way I'd said it the last five times, and the ticket taker would receive my money and hand me a slip of ticket with a disapproving shake of her head.

The taxi drivers rarely understood my destination either, without three or four repetitions—and even then they probably guessed about half the time.

Holding the language capacity and literacy level of a small child day after day, interaction after interaction, started to weigh on us. So, when I went out shopping for apples and came home with three eggplant instead, my wife understood why I needed to go to the bedroom and be alone for an hour.

The steam from my unwanted lunch mocked me with its rise into the cool air as I continued my downcast march of chagrin. My daughter hid her face in my neck, just in case any strangers happened upon us. My arms had grown stronger from all the carrying, but my spirit felt weak. These weren't even the big things. These were the tiniest things in life: ordering food, traveling down the road, dressing my daughter. Why were these things so hard?

On my way into our building the guard called me over and tugged my daughter's jacket down at the waistline. I gave him a smile that could have ricocheted bullets and went inside.

It felt hard, because it was hard, but we also had plenty of opportunities to see the hand of God in the very practical blessings he bestowed on us.

I once invited a colleague over for dinner at our apartment, and before the meal I gave him a tour of the house. When he saw my daughter's bedroom a deep scowl bent across his face. I mentally jumped to a hundred conclusions about the source of his displeasure—the messy state of my daughter's room, the number of stuffed animals she owned, the lack of culturally appropriate nursery decorations—but I understood immediately when he pointed at my daughter's bed, or lack thereof.

She'd slept in a portable crib until she couldn't lay flat from corner to corner. We needed to buy her a bed, but this was beyond our capacity, so until we could think of something better, we'd spread some quilts and blankets in a pallet on the floor.

My colleague glared at the pallet, and then up at me. I explained the situation as best I could. We went on with dinner.

The next day he came over with a stack of advertisements from furniture shops. My daughter slept in a new bed by the end of the day.

God intervened on our behalf like this throughout our early days in the country. He made up for the fact of our helplessness with his mercy and provision—creating space for relationship out of our ineptitude and neediness. We felt protected, even as we winced at the sting of failure.

The one area not dominated by failure in those days was my day job.

Part of the reality of closed-country ministry is that you most often rely on other auspices to get and maintain your visa. Cross-cultural workers formerly considered this to be an unwanted burden—and sometimes we still look at it that way, as a hindrance, wasting our time when we'd rather be doing our real job—but in fact, legitimate employment within a closed country can in and of itself aid ministerial work.

I got a visa for myself and my family through being a teacher. It was my day job. Not only did it provide some income for day-to-day expenses, it provided our housing on the same university campus where my students lived and went to class (incarnation). My day job allowed me to live with the people I hoped to reach, and it gave me a door into their lives.

Teaching conversational English, it turned out, was a lot of fun. I taught huge classes, but for the most part my students were interested. They were learning. And they liked my teaching method. The job was compulsory, but it was an incredible blessing. I didn't have to walk through neighborhoods looking for friends—I could just invite them over after class. Due to my teaching, and the pictures of my wife and daughter I showed in class, and just our general foreignness—many of my students were interested in getting to know us. It really was a great set up.

Of course, once they started coming over, we started tripping over the language and the culture. We offended people because we only offered them a drink once (instead of three or four times). We failed to say their names correctly. And sometimes they wouldn't speak at all. Four of my female students came over, sat on the couch, and watched my wife play with our daughter for two hours, remaining virtually silent, but for an occasional group whisper-fest.

My students would offer to help me, which was great because I wanted to get to know them (plus I really needed help). They helped me find the bank. They took me to try local foods. They were excited to be included in our lives.

On one hand it was so encouraging. These students were, in large part, the reason we picked up and moved overseas. But our interactions with them were all surface-level—borderline hollow in nature—and always so exhausting. Life took so much time, and things that would have been easy back home felt so foreign and confusing.

For example, some students took my wife and daughter to the local kindergarten for a visit. On a break, my daughter had to use the toilet, so she walked down the hall with my wife. When they got to the bathroom, they tilted their heads as they beheld an apparatus neither of them had ever seen before.

"Where's the toilet, Mommy?"

My wife took stock of what she saw: a trough spanning the length of the room, some steps, a bar, some more steps . . .

"How do we use this, Mommy?"

My wife frowned. "I honestly have no idea." She evaluated the contraption a while longer, trying to wrap her mind around its function.

"It's ok, Mommy. I can just hold it."

"Thanks, honey."

Such was the nature of life in those first months.

I felt so inept and frustrated. I was still glad to be there, still intent upon heeding our call. I was still aware that our choice had been worthwhile. Yet, when I considered our mission, my disability within the culture compounded, and it so easily turned into guilt.

Part of our training during our first few months involved a book by Don Everts and Doug Schaupp called *I Once Was Lost*. In it, they describe five thresholds most people need to cross on their journey to becoming a believer[1], and the lessons in that book were very freeing to us.

We came from much smaller notions of what evangelism should be, and what its fruit should look like. We thought evangelism was presenting the gospel in a clear and compelling manner, and it resulted in a harvest of souls. Other types of ministry might classify as "outreach," but they weren't technically evangelism.

In fact, the journey toward faith is a continuum. There are often many steps along the way, and any interaction you have with a non-Christian that moves them further down their path to Jesus absolutely qualifies as evangelism. In fact, the fruit of evangelism might not always be a tearful sinner's prayer. It might be a student who moves from skepticism over the existence of God, to a confidence that at least some kind of God exists. It might look like a young man moving beyond his distrust of the church to make

1. Everts and Schaupp, *I Once Was Lost*, 23–24.

friends with a Christian. There are so many thresholds to cross, and each one deserves a party.

But we didn't know that yet.

We were learning that just being with students was more than ninety percent of the ballgame. And we were learning that since we couldn't make time in our incredibly full schedules, we just had to invite them into what we were already doing.

Some of us watched TV with students, cooked or went out to eat with them, studied with them, went shopping with them. Whatever we were doing, we invited them to come along and help us. Our neediness and vulnerability fertilized the soil for deep relationships.

My family settled on a ministry paradigm that would work for us: some meals with students, some play-dates for our daughter. Most of our plan revolved around hospitality and bringing people into our home. We were still just stumbling through, but at least we had a plan.

Even believing what we believed about evangelism, even having decided on a paradigm, making ourselves get out of the house was still a challenge. At least fifty percent of the time we would give up before we'd made it out the door—afraid someone would grab our daughter and scar her already fragile sense of security, afraid they would chastise us about her clothes, afraid to fail.

I took a deep breath as I laced up my daughter's boots and tucked in her sweatpants. I pulled an extra coat over her already fluffy arms. Everyone out there on the other side of my door stood intent to correct me. I purposed to beat them all.

We walked to the nearby playground and spotted another family. As my daughter dug in the sand, a local grandma passed by and pointed out the extra jacket.

"Too hot!" she said, with a frown.

I laughed out loud.

My wife stayed at the playground with our daughter and I walked back home, struck by something that felt important. As my mind wrapped slowly around the truth, some of the tension in my shoulders began to unwind.

"They love us," I said to myself.

The chiding about my daughter's clothes, which I always received negatively, started to take on a new hue. They corrected us. They corrected us all the time. They corrected us even though nothing was really wrong. Why? Because they felt a need to show their superiority? Of course not. They chided us to show us that they cared about us, about our daughter. They were accepting us. They were loving us.

My wife and daughter burst excitedly into the house.

"Guess what happened!"

She had a big smile on her face—a look of satisfaction that was uncharacteristic for either of us in those days.

She undressed our daughter and explained to me that the other family on the playground had come over to dig in the same sand pit. They had a daughter near the age of our own. The woman turned out to be a stay-at-home-mom, and a pastor's wife. She had a vision to reach out to students on our campus, and a particular burden to start an evangelistic outreach to other moms in the area. She wondered if my wife would be interested in joining her.

All we did was step outside.

And this was our reality in those days: deep struggles with the culture, measuring days according to successes and failures . . . mostly failures, fighting for the tiniest of things, and celebrating the tiniest of things, and all this stretching and contorting beneath a satin sheet of grace.

nine

Unchecked Baggage

I'D HEARD THE STORY of Joseph (the dreamer, not the carpenter) a number of times growing up, but never quite like this.

I remembered Joseph's flamboyant jacket, his Father's disproportionate love for him, his dreams about his brothers and his ill-advised transmission of said dreams to said brothers. I remembered how he kept getting betrayed, and yet somehow kept prospering—as a slave, then a prisoner, then the number two guy in Egypt.[1]

But I'd never thought about Joseph's pain.

What was it like to hold on to dreams from God when he was working as a slave—having been brought low by the very brothers who bowed down to him in his vision? What was it like to carry their betrayal? And after he had moved on with his life, taken an Egyptian wife and had kids and left the memories of his overbearing Father and jealous brothers far behind, what was it like when they showed up at his doorstep begging for food?

How easily we forget the characters in the Bible stories we know by heart were real people, with real emotions.

Joseph's story is about how God sustains, and keeps his promises, but it is also a story about family, and how family can really, deeply, mess us up.

---

1. Gen 37:1—41:57.

As the semester moved along, things were looking better on the outside. We could shop and feed our child on a more or less consistent basis. Our relationships with students and teammates were deepening. We moved beyond our initial culture shock. We had our feet under us.

Right around the time we started to feel settled, as if just to make sure we knew we still had a long way to go, God started raising some issues. He spoke in that quiet, gentle way—the tone he uses when he's showing us our brokenness. God wanted to use us, and that meant he needed to mold us, and that meant trimming some things from our innermost being.

My wife's brokenness revolved largely around homesickness. She had said yes to God's call, but reluctantly. In other words, she had obeyed, but that didn't mean she had to like it. As a stay-at-home mom she didn't have many free moments, but the moments she found were spent at the computer, feeding the longings of her soul with pictures of things she missed back home. She complained a lot in those days. She missed her parents. She missed Western food. Sometimes she blamed me, but mostly she just blamed God. It grew to the point that I generally expected her to be in a bad mood. The times she said something positive about our new home were refreshing, but they were exceedingly rare.

In her mind, we were absolutely and officially done after our two-year commitment. Without realizing it, she gave herself permission not to fall in love with the place, to keep it at a distance, to consider her life on pause for two years. Any other mindset would leave her feeling homesick and sad. This was her brokenness, and it affected every facet of her life.

Contrarily, I was falling more in love with the country every day. I was happy to have left the West behind, and as much as my taste for the local food got under her skin, her failure to acclimate got under mine. She complained. I got angry. We both shut down.

Besides a failure to support and encourage my wife during this difficult time, I exhibited frailty in other ways. My own brokenness took the form of a short temper and an over-sensitive attitude, but God whispered to me that the roots of this had nothing to do with our new country, nothing to do with my wife's behavior, and everything to do with my past.

I knew on some level or another that I had been formed by my past, and that not all of that formation had been positive. But at my age I was far enough removed from childhood that I didn't think it had anything to do with my present situation. Sure, I was the product of a broken home. Sure, both my parents had made a few mistakes—just like everyone else's parents.

The details aren't important because the problem of past pain is not unique to me. Everyone has past pain. You don't have to be a missionary to wrestle with it, and ignoring a call from God won't mean you don't have to deal with it.

But was it really such a big deal? And even if it was, why was it coming up now?

My wife and I remembered a sermon we'd heard in college about the creation of the world—how the Spirit of God hovered over the water, and how the Spirit of God still hovers over the world crying out one of two things. Over the praiseworthy things he cries out in praise; over the darkness he cries back to the Father, "This doesn't look like you!"

Something similar was happening in our hearts. We needed the Spirit to help us engage with the culture and do the ministry he'd called us to do, and the Spirit was faithful to come and to help us. But he was also faithful to call out those things in us that were praiseworthy, and those things in need of change.

Either way, I didn't see why God felt the need to bother me about it when I obviously had other things to deal with, and I told him so. I imagine he got a bit of a kick out of that.

While I did my best to ignore the voice of the Lord, the brokenness I was inadvertently feeding leapt from my heart and into my life like a wet Gremlin after midnight. It crept into every aspect of my day.

I had a conflict with a student after class in which my temper was an issue. I had disturbing dreams that left me feeling confused and angry. I got frustrated with a teammate for inviting students to my house for a meal, then arriving with his food an hour late. A mildly negative reaction to these situations on my part might have been appropriate, but I was responding out of brokenness, and therefore out of proportion.

I also caught myself getting into imaginary, mental debates with people. I would take someone's words—my wife, a teammate, a student—and lock them against my brain with "C" clamps. Then I would proceed to argue them down. I would point out how wrong they were, how they owed me an apology, all because an action or turn of phrase had caught negatively in my mind. Sometimes I would even make these instances up entirely. I would put words in an adversary's mouth—sure that he or she would have said them anyway—and then I would berate him in my head as I washed dishes or walked to class.

That these were the actions of a clinically insane person (rather than a missionary) was not lost on me.

Every time I did this I was sowing to anger rather than peace, judgment rather than forgiveness. It made me feel like a failure, and it built a framework for me to become a very angry person.

Richard Foster writes about coming to God just as we are. When we are walking through a time of wilderness—when we experience the perceived absence of God—he recommends a form of prayer which he calls, "The Prayer of the Forsaken." He focuses on what the wilderness produces in us, and encourages Christians to complain along with the Psalmist, even as we persist in loving and seeking the Father. What we have learned in the light we continue to practice in the dark.[2]

The Prayer of the Forsaken was a comfort to me during those days. In truth, I was not experiencing a time of wilderness; God was quite near and I knew it. But I was ignoring his whisper in my ear,

2. Foster, *Prayer: Finding the Heart's True Home*, 17–26.

running from the issues he wanted to lay bare in my life. So it felt a lot like being in a desert.

The writer of Psalm 71 begs God to be his refuge in a time of suffering. Though he experiences the reproach of men, he clings to God, and the memories of the good things God has done. Even though his enemies are rising up, he says, "But I will hope continually and will praise you yet more and more."[3] And he stands confidently in the goodness of God, crying, "You who have made me see many troubles and calamities will revive me again; from the depths of the earth you will bring me up again."[4]

If God is pleased by our humility and contrite spirit, then we ought not shy away from the things that humble and break us. Maybe we even ought to seek those things out to some degree, that we might know his nearness. The things that break us force us into his refuge, where we are made whole, and where we cannot forget him. This is why even psalms full of suffering still speak a word of trust in the Lord: "I know that God is for me."

The blessings of Joseph are striking when you consider that he never would have stepped into them had it not been for suffering. Had he not been sold, he never would have found himself in Egypt to interpret Pharaoh's dream, saving Egypt and the surrounding lands from famine. Being sold into slavery is tragic, but between his doting father and envious brothers, Joseph wasn't doing all that well at home in the first place. In a sense, God used suffering to rescue Joseph from a poor family situation, and to move him into further fields of blessing.

As I sought God through prayer and the Psalms, I knew that I had to deal with my past pain. I couldn't keep putting it away. Even as I sought to be used by God as a messenger of his deliverance, he, in his great mercy, wanted to deliver me from my troubles.

I was hit very hard with the realization that I was pretty messed up. I knew I was a sinner, of course, but the mission field

3. Ps 71:14 ESV.
4. Ps 71:20 ESV.

had a way of bringing those sins together in a clearly defined point. I found that I was selfish with my time, judgmental toward my wife and teammates. Through relationships my flaws were laid out so that I could plainly see how far I was from perfect, and how the dark places in my past served to produce this broken fruit of sin. It helped to humble me, and push me toward the cross where God might refine me.

But to call the process enjoyable would be a lie.

I knew then, more than any other time in ministry, that I simply could not do it on my own. All that emotional baggage, gone unchecked for years, was finally breaking me down. The system I'd built as a child to sustain me through hard times had worn too thin. I was breaking. If God didn't rescue me soon I would utterly crash and burn.

ten

Slow Walks

THE CRACKS IN MY countenance became more and more apparent, especially to my wife. She often needed a place to vent her frustrations in those days, and she felt free to do this when I appeared strong. But when it became obvious that my spirit was eroding beneath the weight of community and evangelism, the difficulties and foreignness of the culture, and the overall cadence of my spiritual journey, she internalized her darker feelings. She poisoned herself in an effort to spare me the burden.

When I searched for deliverance, it came quietly, subtly, like an easy afternoon walk, like a branch slowly budding from a vine.

In a quiet park tucked within our city, I read these words from John 15:

> I am the vine, you are the branches.
>
> Whoever abides in me, and I in him, he it is who bears much fruit, for apart from me you can do nothing.
>
> If anyone does not abide in me he is thrown away like a branch and withers; and the branches are gathered, thrown into the fire, and burned.
>
> If you abide in me, and my words abide in you, ask whatever you wish and it will be done for you.
>
> By this my Father is glorified, that you bear much fruit and so prove to be my disciples.
>
> As the Father has loved me, so I have loved you. Abide in my love.[1]

1. John 15:5–9 ESV.

Somewhere between meeting new friends, trying to reach out to them, engaging in cultural acquisition, reading assignments from my team leaders, my day job, and the general busyness of life on the edge of the map, I had forgotten to make time for Jesus.

I'd been through plenty of guilty phases in my life involving regimented quiet times, and I'd experienced plenty of self-castigation when my highly regimented quiet times dried up or fell by the wayside. Nevertheless, when I realized my deficit, I tried to implement new standards in my day. I tried to rise early and pray, or stay up late and seek God in his Word. I tried setting time aside here and there, but none of my former patterns—the methods that had served me throughout various stages of my walk with Jesus—none of my trying seemed to bring me any closer to his presence in my new context of life.

I was frustrated, and I soon realized that it wasn't about thirty minutes a day, or three chapters a day, or any manner of quota that needed to be satisfied. I just needed to be with Jesus. He wanted to do a new thing.

On that afternoon in the park he showed me a new way.

We had tried what some call Lectio Divina, or Gospel Meditation—a form of Scripture reading that enlists the imagination. We read the passage several times, meditating on various questions as we listened to the Word. We pictured ourselves in the story, or tried to identify with various characters—depending on the passage. In the case of John 15, we just read it very, very slowly. We split up and meditated through the passage in steps.

For me, that meant a walk to the park with my journal.

"I am the vine; you are the branches."
The branch grows out of the vine. It is a part of the vine. Connected. The branch is not responsible for the depth of its roots or its nutrition—it just receives from the vine. It takes in the light, which tracks back to the vine, but the process is not the responsibility of the branch. The wind blows the branch; it is anchored to the vine. The moth eats the branch; the vine sustains it. The branch bears fruit; the vine supplies it. The branch is simply an extension of the vine.
How is my relationship to Jesus like this? . . .

And so on and so forth through the passage. It took me two hours to process four verses.

By the end of my Scripture meditation, I remembered something that I had forgotten: God loved me. For a while, maybe years, I'd been thinking of the cross as the power of God—a theological victory over death and the enemy. But it was also an act of rescue. Jesus gave up everything for me, to be with me, because he loved me. So much teaching on his holiness had helped me forget about his love—the very foundation from which I should have been ministering and living in the first place. That God loved me should have been the main idea all along, but I'd forgotten.

In that quiet afternoon, God reminded me.

Over the next several months I structured my Sabbaths around an extended period of time in the Word, during which I could be alone and process Scripture at a snail's pace. This method of abiding in Christ was quite new to me, almost like a couple setting aside time for date night. I called these intimate times with Jesus "slow walks."

I pictured myself walking up a hill, where my friend, my teacher, my elder brother was already sitting, waiting for me. He had a thermos of coffee ready for me. We sat down together, and I looked out over green fields and mountains, obscured by the amount of light. Then I listened to him tell me stories.

I would pray and ask God for a Scripture through which to walk. Then I prayerfully journaled through the passage. These meditative times almost always involved an actual walk around the city or around our campus.

One morning, for example, I read through some early psalms. Their words spoke of refuge and rescue and the glory of God. I read them slowly, assessing my thirst for the glory of God, and sensing it grow as I imagined the taste of living water. Then I took a walk around our school. I kept saying to God, "Show me your glory."

As I strolled across a bridge over a small pond, I saw a family of swallows gliding over the water, rising and dipping for pond skaters in a cadence as beautiful as it was complex. God whispered that this was what he saw in our community—a coordinated expedition. "Just do what you were made to do, like these birds," he said, "And you will see what my glory looks like."

As soon as I began implementing this strategy, I was tempted to leave it behind. By the time my Sabbath rolled around I was usually pretty tired. I tried to talk myself into just resting, just watching TV, anything other than keeping my appointment with Jesus. Every time I kept the appointment was a victory; every time I kept the appointment he blessed me.

I particularly enjoyed slow walks through familiar passages. For example, one afternoon I read slowly through the third chapter of Philippians, asking myself questions like, "What things did Paul count as loss?" and "What have I counted loss?" or "What does it even mean to count something as loss?" As I read the words and extrapolated and journaled, I kept coming back to the surpassing value of knowing Christ.

> To know him is everything. Compared to knowing him, everything else is worthless. The gaining of Christ is associated with the de-valuing of all other things. A house is a good thing. Freedom is a good thing. But compared to knowing him they are like trash—something we throw away—or further still, like refuse—something we avoid, something of literally negative value.
>
> And how do we know him? How are we found in him? What does it mean to be found in him? If man's righteousness is like refuse, and the righteousness of God is perfection, how can we look elsewhere? How can we find something better than perfection?

"Do you want to know satisfaction?" God asked. "Then know me."

God encouraged me to seek him, to know him, and as I did so during those slow walks, I caught glimpses of his divine perfection, and the things of earth grew strangely dim. I began to long for eternity, and for the return of Christ, as I never had before.

None of this intimacy generated from me. It didn't seem as though I was becoming more inwardly or outwardly holy. I had no righteousness of my own. I was still incredibly flawed. I still fought and thrashed against his gentle hand. But as I strived to know him, that he was slowly changing me was undeniable.

Those sweet times of Sabbath rest built me up, the way the Sabbath was meant to build us. I laid down the difficulties of community, my failures in culture, and my fears about evangelism. I laid down the brokenness in my past. I sought new life in his Word, in his presence. And like that rippling pool from months before, God filled me with his Spirit—drop after drop, leading to a steady stream—and I knew the ripples of my influence, Christ in me, would eventually have deep effect upon the place I now called home, even as they impacted my own spirit.

God was healing me.

Even though a metaphorical fog still hung over my new life, the Lord was my light. Even as I struggled to understand the culture, even as I fought with my wife and my teammates, even as I confronted personal issues long dormant beneath my skin—the Lord was with me. He was with me in trouble. He was with me in feast. He was whispering that it was worth it—that this call, this refining process, was all in his hands. It was worth it. We would be ok. We would make it.

The book of Psalms promises that God is with us in trouble, but we don't really know that in our bones until we get into trouble. Following God off the edge of the map is a surefire way to learn the truth of his promises. He does not leave us, nor does he forsake us. He is with us.

I walked into the house after a serene stroll through the village near our campus. The heater in our apartment was broken, but I was hot from the walk so I shed the coat I wore against the coming winter. I kissed my daughter, bundled up in a sweater, playing with misshapen blocks in the floor of our living room. I saw my wife, facing out the window before a fading autumn afternoon. I breathed deeply of my home, and my life, satisfied.

Our team was coming over that evening for a worship service, so I set about getting some snacks and coffee ready. My wife joined me with a nervous smile. I looked at her face and thought that perhaps she hadn't had time to prepare the song sheets. Of course, that was no big deal. I smiled to reassure her.

She waited for me to put the coffee down, then stood up straight and looked into my eyes.

"I'm pregnant," she said.

PART THREE

Incubation

eleven

The Trough

CLEAR SKIES STRETCHED ALONG the open ocean—blue color swatches, deep to faint—framed in vibrant tones by tree branches criss-crossing from the mountainside. Perched on a cliff like a resting bird, I stared out over the harbor, at the rainbow of docked fishing boats, dancing in a thousand colors against the sea. From that height, the surf seemed to roll in slow-motion over the small golden beach.

I thanked God for a peek at his majesty, breathed in the sea and the mountain, then gathered my things for the descent.

Our team had traveled to a small island for our winter retreat. It was meant to be a dedicated time of respite from the rigors of missionary life—a time to recharge, and receive some special teaching on evangelism. Because we live and work in a city, we chose a less developed corner of the world for our retreat. And since we spend most of our days behind a wall that restricts religious freedom, we opted for a country with a more liberal bent.

Whenever you leave a country closed to the gospel after an extended stay, a palpable change in atmosphere signals your departure. In the same way that the incense of a temple unsettles, or a dark hallway frightens, the air on our side of the border feels heavy and vacant at once. This sensation is more discernible at some times than others, and heavier in certain places—but when you leave the country, you feel the difference.

As I walked down the mountain, my jolting, downhill gate gave rise to a tick in my knees. First the left, then the right as well. I almost muttered a complaint, but then I remembered my wife, now several months into her pregnancy, who had to walk the same, slippery cobblestone path. Motorized vehicles were outlawed on that particular island, which was an awesome idea until we realized that to get anywhere we had to walk at least twenty minutes uphill or downhill at a decent grade. My pregnant wife was not thrilled about this.

The pregnancy had been a complete surprise, and to be honest, I didn't feel ready for another baby at all. The waves of newness rising and crashing against my sandy frame saw a tremendous adjustment to the shoreline of my identity—and now rushed in the tide. Memories of exhaustion and exasperation flooded my heart, and I doubted once again that God had any idea what he was doing with us.

He was faithful, of course. An obscure verse of the old hymn "It is Well With my Soul" spoke peace to me: "For me be it Christ, be it Christ hence to live / If Jordan above me shall roll / No pain shall be mine, for in death as in life / Thou wilt whisper thy peace to my soul."[1]

The words aren't about having a baby; they're about death. But kids can be a kind of death. Children—just like marriage, or moving—signal an end to one way, a former idea of life, even as they usher in a new one. And this new one is better, of course, but we don't always know that on the front side.

I found my feet after some prayer. I saw the ways God had been preparing us. The baby would come mid-summer, right at a break in my teaching schedule, a mere week or two after the pregnancy clause of our health insurance took effect. His hand was evident. It was well with my soul and I would not be shaken. I would not be moved.

I slipped on a patch of gravel and almost went head over heels down the mountain path, finally muttering the complaint that had been on my heart all along. I brushed sandy pebbles and bits of

1. Spafford, "It Is Well With My Soul."

paint from my knees and took in the homes that lined the narrow stretch of road: cracked plaster, painted over several times, probably against the weather in the harsher months; rusted lines of fence and gardening tools littering tiny plots in front of the barely kept houses; the lone, winding path, missing stones here and there, veined by slices of water and time.

I trudged on toward the beach, the ache in my knees a bit hotter, so aware of my own exhaustion.

Winter retreat hadn't come soon enough. The months of teaching and cultural acquisition and community building, not to mention round after round in a boxing ring with demons from my past had left me bruised and stripped. My brokenness, my frailty, confronted me on a daily basis, each day louder than the one before. Slowly, I'd stopped trying to minister or thrive; I'd settled on just trying to survive. I desperately needed a break on a quiet island.

My wife was the same, or worse, depending on the day, and our condition was taking a particular toll on our marriage. There were days in which our shared sufferings might have brought us together if we'd allowed it, but more often than not we failed to bond, retreating instead, aching privately, bristling corporately. We didn't yet know how to hurt together. In his goodness, God was trying to allow our circumstances to grow us toward each other. Up to that point, however, we weren't getting it.

The ground beneath me finally leveled out as I completed my descent at the pier. Up close, the colors of the fishing boats lapped dully one to the next, the distant memory of their brilliance a fading mirage. Fish scales collected against the crumbling seawall. The air—formerly a mixture of mountains and sea—sat heavy with the stench of fish and fishermen.

A few steps from the pier, the sands of the beach grew black with tar and other pollutants. The water spat gray foam against what might have been used coffee grounds. I looked up at the mountain, down at the corrupt sands, and I hung my shoulders in the face of that place. It was an ugly place. A place I wanted to leave as soon as possible.

On this island, as in life, everything hinged on the point of view.

The mountain and the valley—this was the experience of our winter retreat.

One of the high points was our focus: evangelism.

We brought in an experienced evangelist who spent several sessions helping us process issues raised by our host culture and strategizing different methods of engagement. We encouraged each other with shared experiences and the shared desire to open the Bible with our students. After a full semester we'd been successful in building many friendships, but thus far no one had been curious enough about Jesus to investigate the Bible with us. Faith that we would share the story of Jesus with our friends next semester rose up in us as we prayed and encouraged each other.

Our friends also prayed for our personal needs. That we were feeling weary and troubled was no secret to our team, and they cast precious words of blessing over our family during the conference.

For my wife, they prayed from 2 Corinthians: "My grace is sufficient for you, for my strength is made perfect in weakness."[2] They encouraged her to trust in the goodness of God—that he had not invited her off the edge of the map only to abandon her. They reminded her that nothing could separate her from God's love, and prayed she would discover depths of this love yet unknown to her. She needed to hear these words. She needed to take her eyes off her circumstances, and set them on the love of Christ.

Most of their prayers for me focused on rest—that I would find a more steady balance between work and rest, and keep trusting God to bring our labor to fruition. They said I'd been walking on a ridge line, high on a misty mountain, and that God was with me, but there weren't many colors on the path. They prayed that I would withstand the enemy's lies about my identity, and rely on God's strength to sustain me. They prayed that I would endure, and believe that soon God would lead me down into the valley, a place bursting with color and life.

2. 2 Cor 12:9a NKJV.

Hopeful prayers. They acknowledged our state, but pushed us to see beyond. We left those times of prayer feeling spiritually full, and at peace . . . for a while.

On the other hand. We were physically ill for almost the entirety of our stay on the island.

Our daughter was the first to catch the bug. She complained of a stomach ache before bed on the first night, and by morning she had thrown up six times. I caught a milder version of the same thing a day later. My wife caught it last, and worst of all.

On the free day of our conference, most of the team went snorkeling or exploring in a cave. I walked my nauseated, pregnant wife down the forty-five minute descent (twenty minutes if you're healthy and not with child) to the only medical clinic on the island where she got an I.V.

God was calling us to rest, and to learn to rest. He was inviting us to praise him in spite of circumstances. He drew near, but we were mentally and physically falling apart. We were sick for nine out of ten days on the island. Instead of rest we felt exhaustion; instead of quiet we heard vomiting.

Maybe the sickness was a kind of metaphor for our spiritual state, and especially the state of our marriage. We were sick, tired, and vomiting, nearly writhing in pain as what was inside came to the surface. We could let it out, heal, and move forward, or we could choke it back, ignore our problems, and remain broken.

Our leaders gave us some good counsel (in between trips to the bathroom) which we tried to hold to and apply. We were not the first to go through this, nor would we be the last. The up-hill paths we faced were well trodden, common to most every missionary family that had come before us. We tried very hard to believe and take solace in this. But we were quite literally running on empty.

For my part, even once the sickness passed, a kind of guilt remained because my wife had it worse. Guilt chased me even in rest, maybe especially in rest. Aware of my struggle with guilt and notions of purpose, I found myself wondering as I cleaned the bathroom floor, was life supposed to be so hard? So much pressure? So much effort? If life was a gift, why did I spend it feeling inadequate—like I ought to be doing so much more with it?

Edge of the Map

I had followed God off the edge of the map, but it didn't feel like enough. God wasn't telling me this, of course. I was telling it to myself. It was like walking a colorless road.

Toward the end of our stay on the island, a teammate offered to tend to my wife and daughter for an hour so I could take a walk. I was grateful, and also a little ashamed that I had so obviously reached the end of my strength. I knew I should cut my wife some slack. After all, she was passing through the same trials of work in a closed country, only amplified by being sick and pregnant. She wrestled with guilt about moving far away from her parents, and she was so very tired. I knew all of this, but I was so worn from months of complaint about the weather and the food and the culture, my compassion had run out. And I hated myself for that. I sat down on a bench, plagued with guilt and regret, and prayed a horrible, selfish prayer.

I told God I couldn't handle it anymore. He was going to have to do something, soon. I told him it was hard enough leaving a life and building a life and joining a team and learning a culture, and that I needed my wife on my side—not contending against me with every other breath. I confessed to him the anger and resentment. I told him I didn't believe his strength was being perfected in my present weakness, and I wanted out. I told him that I wished he would just go ahead and take me to heaven, because I was pretty much ready to give up.

And so on and so forth.

I journaled my thoughts, read over them, felt terrible, and went home.

In my youth, I would have expected God to be angry, or at least disappointed by my lack of faith and perseverance. But our God hears terrible, selfish prayers like mine, and responds with gentle love.

We met an Irish couple at dinner that night, guests at the same hostel on the island. We learned that they were retired missionaries to India and they offered to pray for us. I was in a bad mood, and

I honestly didn't want to explain our situation to some strangers, but I couldn't really refuse prayer, so after dinner the four of us sat down in a quiet living room and talked.

The couple—Jim and Billie—were two of the sweetest people I had ever met. Their wrinkles told of a life of smiles and laughter, and also pain. They were wise, and so tender with my wife, and they prayed things for me that made me regret my earlier attitude.

They recognized that my wife was depressed, on top of which she was pregnant, on top of which she was in the "trough."

"Missionary life is full of ups and downs," they said. "But you're almost never as low as you are during the first six months. That's the trough. The lowest point."

The trough doesn't make it into the missions brochure.

We weren't prepared for the trough, but somehow just hearing it articulated by another missionary couple, just being authorized to admit that things were low, made it better. Not a lot better right away, but a little better.

Jim and Billie gave my wife some great advice about how to rest. They didn't judge her. They looked at her the same way God looked at her—with compassion. They reminded me of her beauty, and encouraged me to be strong and pray for her.

We loved that couple dearly, though we only knew them for an hour. I was so grateful to God for having responded to my complaint with the gift of two Irish saints. After some prayer, and some more talking, we had hope. Our road was challenging, but God believed in us. He'd called us, after all, knowing our weaknesses and shortcomings full well. After our failed attempt to rest on a quiet island, our marriage began to strengthen.

Still, the residual pain in my knees and the eerie vision of a colorless ridge stayed with me. I had a sense there were some hard days yet to come.

twelve

City Relics

THE SHADOW OF MY kneeling form trembled with the bend of the candles in the solitary room. Warm light glanced across the walls while the air of bread and wine and candle wax filled my lungs. The rug, the small end-table, the Bible and the journal—all glowed a deep, deep red.

We were in the middle of a twenty-four hour prayer vigil for our campus, and the small office was heavy with a heavenly presence. Even as I'd entered the room I almost burst into tears at the sense of power, the hours spent in prayer, the voices of angels crying out the glory of our Maker. Now, as I rose from communion, his nearness was just as palpable.

The headlights of a passing car caught my attention and I strode to the window. The contrast between light and dark obscured my vision of the campus. The dormitories and sidewalks and classrooms I might have seen in the daylight all fell dim, blurred by the street lamps warring against the night. I blinked my eyes and took stock of the light—an irregular span of lamps lined a sidewalk, curving back toward the dorms; an occasionally lit window stood out against the majority of darkened homes; a singularly bright work lamp shone out from the top of a factory in the distance. From my vantage point, the lights made a path—dim to great—from the street, through the student housing, culminating in that powerful star.

I thought of how my Father had ordered my steps, and I prayed for the advance of his kingdom in the words of Isaiah the prophet: "The people who walked in darkness have seen a great light; those who dwelt in a land of deep darkness, on them has light shown."[1]

We'd set the time aside specifically to lift up our students, the vast majority of whom had heard nothing more of Jesus than the occasional picture of a baby in a manger at Christmastime. Most assumed Santa Claus was either the grandfather of Jesus, or Jesus himself as an old man. It sounded silly—almost incomprehensible to a team of Westerners, each raised within a mile of a church in any direction—but this was our new reality.

When you live off the edge of the map, it's not uncommon to find communities that have lived with deep ignorance or err toward the realities of the spiritual world for hundreds, or even thousands of years. This way of life compounds over time, generation after generation, until the better part of a nation thinks life is about financial security and social status, and that existence is an accident. God speaks into this reality. His Spirit hovers over the void. His kingdom advances, bringing life to the barren places, one street lamp at a time.

We prayed in shifts, calling students out by name before the Lord, asking him to stir curiosity. Even before the vigil was over, various team members were approached by students who expressed interest in studying the Bible. That God wanted to move—that he was already moving—was undeniable.

More of Isaiah's prophecy resonated through my brain: "For I will pour water on the thirsty land, and streams on the dry ground. I will pour my Spirit upon your offspring, and my blessing on your descendants. They shall spring up among the grass like willows by flowing streams. This one will say, 'I am the Lord's.'"[2]

That's what we prayed for: a move of the Spirit.

1. Is 9:2 ESV.
2. Is 44:3–5a ESV.

My favorite parable is without question the parable of the seed in the fourth chapter of Mark.

> The kingdom of God is as if a man should scatter seed on the ground. He sleeps and rises night and day, and the seed sprouts and grows; he knows not how. The earth produces by itself, first the blade, then the ear, then the full grain in the ear. But when the grain is ripe, at once he puts in the sickle, because the harvest has come.[3]

It's a story of how the kingdom grows, and the best part is, of course, it happens in this mysterious way that we cannot comprehend. It grows beneath the earth, while we are sleeping and waking and going about the business of our lives—it grows, and we know not how.

I don't mean to suggest that we shouldn't have strategies, I'm simply pointing out that the beauty of the process is its mystery. If we knew how it worked, we could break it. And we would. But we don't know how it works. This parable is incredibly freeing in the context of evangelism.

Formerly, I carried so much stress and weight any time I tried to transmit the gospel, so much pressure. I was so afraid of being rejected, and so afraid that my poor attempt would push someone even further away from faith, and that one day I'd have to answer to the throne of grace for being such an idiot to have shared my faith in the first place.

I was somehow set free by knowing that I couldn't break it down into parts, and that even though there was definitely a process (first the blade, then the ear, etc.), it was a process that I couldn't fully comprehend, and for which I was mostly not responsible.

Sharing the gospel ought to be natural, like a seed taking root and sprouting. It ought to be the most natural thing in the world. If we're in touch with how good the news is, and how good Jesus is, we won't feel the need to package him—to don the suit of a used car salesman, talking up the pros and downplaying the cons. Jesus is beautiful, and plenty intriguing all by himself.

3. Mark 4:26–29 ESV.

Yet, like competent farmers, we are also supposed to have eyes for the whiteness of the harvest. Timing is of great importance in this parable. The farmer takes out the sickle "at once" when the harvest has come. There is an urgency, and it is in tension with the process of the harvest, the need to wait for the grain to ripen.

As we prayed for students and sought them out, we asked God to be near, and for the gospel to fill our mouths in the most natural way. We prayed for discernment about the soil—in whom we ought to invest, and how to go about it. We prayed for the eyes of seasoned farmers: eyes for the harvest.

We trusted God. We waited.

As students came, we began to encounter, with them, their barriers to faith.

Some of their barriers were similar to ones we might have crossed in the West. A need to please others, for example, and a fear of what others might think about them if they were to take faith seriously. In honor/shame-based cultures, however, this need for societal approval is highly intensified. So, where individuality and uniqueness might be prized in the West, here they were eschewed. Everyone wanted to fit with the majority. They needed to fit. Their discomfort outside of the majority was ethereally intense.

Societal pressures, familial pressures, financial and academic pressures: The cards were stacked heavily against our students even having time to consider God—much less making a decision to follow him.

A staggering reality of ministry in a closed country is how long evangelism can take. As a foreigner, building trust takes time even when you know the culture, and even more time when you don't. No amount of preparation or strategizing can take the place of this time. You must invest in people. Like a farmer, you just have to learn to wait.

That waiting was hard for us. On a particularly dreary day I took a walk to the sports stadium on our campus. Class was in session so the arena which might have held thousands was entirely empty but for me. I watched the sun rise quickly and then glide across half the sky, failing to burn off the fog in that empty place, and I felt that no one wanted the light I held, and that my efforts at relationship building and evangelism would come to nothing. It was a lie, of course, but one I whispered often during those winter days.

On many occasions like this I fell victim to a quiet temptation: To equate the message, and its acceptance or denial, with my own identity. The more resistance we met, the more I believed my identity wrapped in failure. Discouragement I could scarcely discern chipped away at my spirit.

When I got downhearted like that, I knew I needed to retreat and be with Jesus.

I asked him to fill that stadium with worshipers. I asked him to shine and burn the fog away. I asked him to show us true reality, and to expose the lies for what they were. I asked him to purify me, that I might speak his wonders to those who had yet to know their author.

Chloe was a student in my English class, but I didn't formally meet her until my friend Michael came to visit me from the U.S. Michael stayed with us for a few weeks, and took part in our classes and prayer meetings and parties. One morning, Michael asked my class if any of the students wanted to go with him to visit some ancient relics in the city. Chloe was among the students who volunteered.

I accompanied Michael and Chloe and a few students to the city relics on a Saturday afternoon. Most of the students came to practice their English, and hang out with Michael, but Chloe was a bit different. She had prepared pages and pages of information about the relics, and spent the afternoon acting as our tour guide. She pointed out different architectural structures—which happened to be part of her major in school. She translated the signs and descriptions, and helped us try some local food. She was particularly interested in the local minority religion, and told us a lot about that as we toured the relics.

On the long bus ride back to campus, Chloe and I had a conversation about religion. She had no faith, herself, but didn't seem opposed to it. She told me she liked reading English books, and when I told her about my favorite book, the Bible, she casually mentioned that she might be interested in reading it.

"Dude," Michael said later, "You've totally got to ask her to study with you." He had been listening to our conversation on the bus.

I agreed with him, but expressed a little trepidation. I had only just met Chloe after all, and I wasn't sure if she was ready.

"Whatever, man. You need to ask her."

Friends from out of town like Michael were a rare treat for us in those days. Few found the time or money to make it to our neck of the map, but when they came, they brought us something we needed desperately—fresh eyes. Michael was right, of course. Chloe seemed pretty open, and I had been praying for students to approach me about Bible study. So I made a plan.

I invited Chloe out for dinner to thank her for being Michael's tour guide. My plan was to bring up the Bible during our conversation, but we finished dinner and walked back to my house for coffee and I just couldn't find a way to raise the topic. As my minutes slipped away I sipped my coffee, feeling more and more like a failure. Then the strangest thing happened.

My daughter took a picture-book off of the shelf in her room, came into the living room, and sat down in the floor. She read out the pictures, enjoying the attention as we listened to her. Then Chloe asked her the name of the book.

"It's my Bible," she said, pointing to a picture of Jesus lying in a manger.

I took that as a sign.

After a brief and quite natural conversation, Chloe agreed to study the Bible with me once a week.

She left having enjoyed the food and the company, and having no idea of the prayers God had answered through her that night. She was the first student with whom I would read the Bible as evangelism. She was drawn by the Holy Spirit to hear the message. I found myself thinking over and over, "This one will say, 'I am the Lord's.'"

thirteen

The Comfortable Lie

I THINK ONE OF the reasons we often stumble into temptation is the subtlety with which sin can creep up on us. One moment we are going about our day, business as usual, and in the next moment we are sinning, almost without having noticed until we are wrapped in it. Our busyness may be part of the problem, but the point is that though sin was not originally part of our nature, it has been grafted into our psyche over centuries, so that now, to sin can feel quite natural indeed, like putting on a worn pair of jeans.

Then again, sometimes temptation cries out in a voice so foreign we can scarcely make out its accent.

The dark whispers began as I sat in class, listening to students give group presentations. Each group spoke for ten minutes about different universities elsewhere in the world where they might study as foreign exchange students. As I watched them show slides of the spires of Cambridge, I caught my mind drifting away to a former dream.

You could have joined the Ivy League. You had the grades. You still could . . .

Academia was a dream I'd romanticized for a time and then left behind. I had quite happily forsaken that aspiration for other things I loved more, so I was surprised to feel such a longing for the bricks and towers and old books creeping up my leg like a vine of ivy.

Knowledge matters. You could succeed there. They would respect you there . . .

The next slide showed some students at a coffee shop. More likely they were models posing as students because they were all physically stunning. They smoked and sipped coffee and laughed, and I felt a temptation of another kind wind similarly through me.

See their beauty. See their ease. This could be yours if you choose it.

My eyes drifted over the students in my class and, quite suddenly, I sat upright. It was as if the class and the presentation and the students froze in time, and I was alone in my seat. A singular awareness struck me: I was listening to the enemy's slippery voice.

As I sat back from the desk and recalled the journey my mind had taken, it was almost comically obvious how the enemy had reached out to me—first through pride of vocation, then through lust. I stopped listening to the presentation and started journaling. I wrote down what the enemy was whispering, and prayed prayers to counter the temptation.

Yes. Write it down. In fact, write a book. You could teach others if you write a book. You could be great. Your name would be known. Just spend your time writing . . .

I was so shocked by the boldness of the tempter that I laughed out loud. The student giving her presentation paused, looking up briefly at my outburst. I shook my head and continued writing.

The whispers of the enemy in that class were so clear, yet so foreign. Temptation didn't feel natural in that moment; it felt like another language, another life. I called my wife on the way back from class and we prayed together that I would flee temptation.

Sometimes, when we're on mission, the voice of the enemy stands out like this, and it is a grace to us. We have the opportunity to recognize it for the lie that it is, and flee temptation before it can wrap itself around us. It isn't about fighting, really. It's about running. We run to the light like children, who innately understand its power to scatter the darkness.

Other times, the voice of the enemy glows with something so near the truth, something so familiar and comfortable, that we can dream hours away in a lie without ever waking up. For me, the comfortable lie had to do with my identity.

As a team we processed our self-concept together. We made lists to answer the question, "Who are you?" We gave answers like, "I am a Father," or, "I am a Teacher." The point of the exercise was to recognize that though we did many things and occupied many roles, our truest identity was our place in the family of God. More than the fact that we were servants, more than the reality that we were sinners saved by grace, we were sons and daughters of the King.

This was true.

We put it on paper.

We believed it.

But lies had also burrowed into my identity like rats. They'd made a home in me long ago, so that I could no longer pick them out from the rest of my internal furniture. Lies about my worth and adequacy ran through me like the double-helix ran through my cells. I was not good enough, and I had known it for so long that I couldn't be talked out of believing it. It didn't feel like a lie. It felt just like home to me.

The trappings of the mission field cater to this self-concept. We begin to equate ourselves—our worth—with our success. And we may not see a lot of success (in its traditional sense) when we are starting out in a closed country.

As my friends and mentors on the field began to point this out in me, we realized together that this and other lies had a lot to do with past pain. The realization—obvious to everyone but me—was not that I had pain in my past, but that said pain was a current issue. From where did my angry outbursts come? From where did my battles with guilt and self-worth arise? They were woven into my foundation—a mess of cracked concrete slab and weeds and bitterness. I set about some reading and journaling assignments designed to expose the lies.

Venom is poisonous, which, I suppose is obvious. Just as poisonous words seep into and infect those upon whom we cast them, so venomous thoughts can poison us—slowly taking over and immobilizing our mind and our will, that we might eventually be consumed.

That there would be pain was a promise, but I purposed early on to avoid venom in my words and thoughts as I delved into the past. As I started asking myself hard questions through which to process my past pain, I purposed not to blame my parents or my circumstances, even as I tried to figure out why I was so broken.

Most of those days I felt like a stone, jagged and seemingly without use—certainly without beauty. Even as that felt true, I was also aware that Jesus had stooped in the sand to pick me up, to shape me, to lay me in the house he was building, making me beautiful, purposeful, an important part of something.

The details and facets of my own brokenness could fill another book, but the point is this: When you follow God off the edge of the map, things get raised. Winter is a necessity in the life of any tree. He shows us our scars, and we don't know how to ask him for healing other than to just ask him. It's a painful process, and we have to choose it. And there's life on the other side.

After Chloe and I finished reading the story of the paralyzed man lowered into the house by his friends,[1] Chloe sat back and said, "So, Jesus gives a reproach to the proud people, but he heals the helpless."

She'd been making connections like that and they energized my soul. I'd never seen a non-Christian realizing truths of the gospel on her own. I'd never just sat back and watched the Bible work. It was amazing.

She sipped her coffee and said, "I think maybe God sent you here."

She said it matter-of-factly, as though it was the most normal thing in the world to suggest. And she was right, of course, but what she probably didn't understand was that God hadn't just sent me there to study the Bible with her; he'd sent me there to be healed.

I was the paralyzed man.

1. Mark 2:1–12.

I don't mean to suggest that I couldn't have found healing back home, but why would I have looked for healing amidst such comfort and ease?

Off the edge of the map I needed healing, and I was willing to fight through some pain to get it.

In my oral English class, I asked a test question for which each student had to prepare a one-minute answer: "What are some qualities of your generation?"

My student Sarah began her answer like most of her classmates. She talked about patriotism and pressure, but then she summed up her statement with these words, "We all just feel like we aren't good enough."

Suddenly it became very personal for me. Suddenly I saw how God had orchestrated my surroundings to force me to deal with my issues. I recognized that if I found redemption from my former notions of self-worth, I would have a very relevant message to offer my students.

And it came up again and again. Whether I was reading stories of healing with Chloe, or studying the sermon on the mount with my teammates, the Holy Spirit kept raising a flashlight to the cavernous breaks in my foundation. My own healing was expressly connected to healing for my students, and the advance of the kingdom in my present context. God was weaving a tapestry. Slowly, I started to get the picture.

Over a long weekend the men on our team climbed a mountain together. We spent most of the day climbing to the top and stayed in a cabin overnight. We played some card games together. We ate free-range chicken and wild rabbit (which tasted suspiciously similar). We retreated together and talked about our identity as sons of God.

I took a short walk alone, beneath a small ridge. Everything was the same color in the light of the setting sun and I recalled my vision of a colorless hike on a mountain. Amidst the quietness and the sunset and the mosquitos I felt God draw near. In that moment he spoke something of my worth to me, but I couldn't really receive it. I was still floundering in the murky waters of my past, and I just didn't feel ready. I felt like the writer of Psalm 139, "Such knowledge is too wonderful for me; it is high; I cannot attain it."[2]

Nevertheless, God spoke in a firm voice, "You are my son." Then the sun dipped behind the mountain, and night began to fall.

As I walked back to the cabin I felt a kind of regret. God had spoken, but I hadn't really taken it in. I'd heard, but I hadn't really received. I knew it because I didn't really feel like a son of God. I still felt inadequate.

When I rounded a bend, the light stung my eyes and I realized that the sun had not set at all. In fact, it had only ducked behind the ridge, and as I walked on, the evening grew warm and orange again. It was as if God was saying, "I know you don't get it yet. But it's true, and you will in time."

It was a very sweet promise.

Near the cabin was a small shrine, smelling of ash and incense. The seven-year-old son of one of our teammates noted the altar and said, "Hey, that's where they pray to their false gods!"

The hairs on my neck stood up as I imagined having to fight off some local worshiper whom he'd offended, but then I realized none of the people around us spoke enough English to have taken offense.

"Do you want to go check it out?" I asked.

He thought about it for a minute, then he said, "Nah. Nobody wants to worship that guy."

I smiled at the notion, so grateful that the God whom I worship is the maker of the mountain, the God of the rising and the setting sun; that he speaks in warm tones, so contrary to the whispers of the enemy; that he is a builder of remarkably intricate things, of which I am one among many; that his truth dissolves the comfortable lie; that he uses us in the midst of our brokenness, and in so doing, leads us to healing.

2. Ps 139:6.

fourteen

Evening Tea

I RECOGNIZED EXACTLY TWO out of the seven dishes on the table: boiled shrimp, and a vegetable I'd seen before, but couldn't name. My wife and I tried not to shuffle in our seats as our hosts smiled at us around their dinner table. We waited patiently for them to teach us how to eat.

The invitation had come as a surprise. One of my students was also a teacher on our campus. She had a daughter about the same age as ours. When I'd told the class my wife was pregnant, Angie came up after class and excitedly invited my family to her home for dinner. "Our daughters can play, and my mother and I will cook for you!"

Angie's mother lived with her and helped take care of their two-year-old. I'd never met Angie's family, but we bought some gifts and showed up on time, happy to try a home-cooked local meal.

My daughter did her best to sit still at the dinner table as we looked at the food. That lasted about one-and-a-half minutes. Then she slipped out of her chair and went back to playing with toys in the living room floor. My wife and I chuckled nervously.

Our hosts smiled and dug into the food. They explained that three of the dishes were especially important for pregnant women to eat as often as possible. My wife did her best, but the flavors were so foreign and the contents so mysterious that it was all she could do to keep the food down. Angie and her husband had this uncanny ability to eat fish—popping it in their mouths, swallowing the meat, spitting out a tiny collection of bones. When we tried a mouthful, we spit out what little meat we'd managed to chew, and the bones drove between our teeth. We showed our bloody smiles as we winced with each bite.

Eating dinner was a harrowing experience.

After the general pace of the meal was set, Angie posed a question: "So, when did you two decide to become Christians?"

A fish bone caught in my throat and I coughed for about two minutes, which was fortunate because I needed time to think.

When you work in a closed country, and the possibility of being spied on is daily present, you learn to exercise caution, especially in the early stages of a relationship.

My wife and I were caught totally off guard. We stumbled through our testimonies as we picked fish bones from our teeth. Our hosts smiled and nodded.

"We're very interested in faith," Angie said. "Of course, we will never believe in God, but did you know my mother is a Christian too?"

She gestured to her quiet mother at the end of the table, smiling as her teeth crunched down on a shrimp head.

My wife and I stole a knowing glance at each other. Angie and her husband John likely had no idea how many times her mother had prayed for them, for a moment like this to happen around her dinner table. And though her mother spoke not a word of English, she certainly understood what was happening that night.

After dinner we heard the girls laughing in a back room so we went to investigate. When we found them, they were tucked into bed together, pretending to be asleep. They threw off the covers, screamed, and laughed at the top of their lungs. John and I smiled and left them to their games.

He gestured for me to sit down in the living room and brought out some tea.

Now, where I come from, we drink coffee. Tea is for old ladies or little girls with stuffed animals. I like many different kinds of coffee and I dislike many different kinds of tea.

But I'd learned a few things about culture and hospitality, so I accepted his offer, fully prepared to hate it with a smile.

John spoke very little English, but we worked out a conversation as he boiled the water. He explained to me where the tea was harvested, and which regions enjoyed which variations of tea. He was an expert on tea.

He brewed it in a pot smaller than the one my daughter used as a toy, and poured the steaming liquid into dainty cups that we had to hold between two fingers. We made for a comical picture—two guys, on a sofa, drinking tiny cups of tea. I took my cue from him, and sipped my tea.

I loved it. Right away, I loved it.

"Good for . . ." he searched for a word, then just pointed at my stomach. I intuited his meaning pertained to digestion, but of course he could have meant it was a constipation remedy, or a diarrhea remedy, or good for a pregnant woman, or something having to do with weight loss . . . He could have meant a lot of things, actually.

We drank about four more pots of tea and by the end of the night my blood pulsed with so much caffeine that I practically floated home. I didn't sleep all night, mostly from the caffeine, but also because of the blessing. We had seen God move around a dinner table, and in a child's bedroom, and over a tiny pot of tea.

Even as scenes like this increased in our lives, as we came to explore the culture further and found things to love, we also sensed a disconnect, growing with equal strength. It wasn't just our inability to chew fish properly. There was a cultural divide, a canyon we couldn't cross, and as we stared into it we grew less and less sure of ourselves.

My wife had been faithfully attending an outreach for young mothers hosted by the pastor's wife she'd met on the playground months before. Her presence initially served as a kind of draw, a foreign attraction so other moms would become interested in the group. By coincidence my wife, the host, and another woman in the group all became pregnant at the same time.

My wife and I recognized God's timing in the pregnancy, and by this time we were excitedly looking forward to the new addition to our family.

The pastor's wife was less enthusiastic about her own condition. Unplanned pregnancy was a big deal in her culture—especially since she already had a daughter—and she was terribly afraid to tell her parents about the pregnancy. Still, she was resigned to trust God and hope for the best.

The third woman in the group was not a believer. She already had a daughter, and she was just as uncomfortable with the societal pressure surrounding unplanned pregnancy. My wife and her friend the pastor's wife prayed for the woman, they talked to her about God's design and the blessings of raising a child, but in the end, she made the culturally acceptable choice and aborted the child.

Even as we picked out names for our new baby, we were forced to mourn a life that would never be. We felt such a disconnect from the culture in times like these, and we realized that we wouldn't want to cross that canyon, even if we could.

Inspired by my newfound love for local tea, John took me to a specialized tea shop. We spoke in broken English as he drove me down back alleys, through open air markets, to the underside of a run-down shopping mall—like we were on the market for something other than tea leaves.

The basement level of the mall boasted a fragrant collection of tea sellers, grouped by price and flavor. John schooled me in the process, which was very specific: "The seller will offer you two cups of one type of tea first, then two cups of a better quality tea, then two cups of the original tea. If you ask for more, it means you want to negotiate the price. You can tell me if you like it, but don't act too enthusiastic . . ." And so on.

The tea shops played out exactly like John had said. The sorters took note of my white skin—uncharacteristic in this local market—then went back to the dried leaves in their hands. The richest leaves they put aside for the tea seller; the stems and broken leaves they collected in a big bag (presumably to be shipped to America).

My newfound addiction to tea notwithstanding, six cups of strong tea in six different shops sent my body into a visible jitter. I shook from seller to seller, high on leaves. I would have gone into debt over tea if John hadn't been there to restrain me. Even so, I spent nearly every dollar in my pocket and walked out with bags and bags of various kinds of tea.

Even in something as small as a cup of tea, this cultural acquisition helped. The canyon of dissonance was still present, but as we adopted the ways and customs and flavors of our neighbors one sip at a time, little by little we began to feel at home.

My Bible study with Chloe had progressed nearly to the point of invitation. We'd read stories about Jesus, talked about how his teaching influenced the lives of his followers, and related the lessons to our present context. Chloe told me she'd randomly met a Christian student who had invited her to a local church, and she had accepted.

I could hardly contain my excitement. My prayers for Chloe, our study together, all of our conversations were finally coming to a head. She would see others worshipping Jesus in her own culture and that would seal the deal.

I just knew it.

What happened instead was nearly the opposite. Chloe felt very uncomfortable in the presence of other Christians from her own culture. She felt pressured by them. Before the meeting was over, she had been significantly burned.

"They wanted me to sign this paper," she told me. "They were all talking and pressuring me, so I signed a paper that says I believe. But I don't." Tears formed in her eyes, but never fell. "But Jesus is something I can believe in my heart, when I'm ready, not what I sign on a paper, right?"

I was proud of her, and I was so disappointed in that church. I'd wanted her to believe so badly. I'd trusted that local church to present the gospel in a culturally relevant way that would cause Chloe to run to Jesus with open arms. Instead, their method had pushed her away.

Chloe still wanted to continue with our Bible study and I was grateful. Still, I found myself in a very uncomfortable place with the local church. I wanted to trust them. I wanted to serve them. I didn't want to feel superior to them—but I did, even in all my brokenness. I felt such disappointment in the way they'd handled my friend. I felt so protective of Chloe, like her journey of faith was my responsibility, my seed to water and tend and protect.

Of course, this notion was mostly untrue. God was in charge of Chloe's journey. He could move through or in spite of the well-meaning missionary or the well-meaning local church. I knew this truth, but in my brokenness, I often forgot it.

Baptism into a foreign culture is often less like baptism and more like learning to swim. You always start in the shallow water—things like fish bones and conversations with taxi drivers—but if you're really going to learn how to swim, you eventually head for the deep water—things like societal opinions on abortion, and the evangelism style of the local church. Experiencing the deep water of foreign culture is like drinking tea in the evening: exhilarating, and often delicious, yet it often steals your sleep as you tremble through the night.

Week by week, we felt the stakes rise.

fifteen

Deterioration

EVERYTHING EXUDED WARMTH—FROM THE air in my apartment, to the steaming mug of milk tea in my hands, to the swell of my heart as I sat beside Chloe on the couch. It was as if we were set aside from the winter, together with the Bible and the presence of the Holy Spirit. I sat on the edge of the cushion with anticipation as my wife prayed for Chloe in the adjoining room.

Chloe and I had studied the life of Jesus together. We'd read his teachings and claims; we'd examined his death and resurrection. Chloe knew it was true, and I knew that she knew. All that remained was for her to stand and be counted as a follower of Jesus.

"So, I have to confess with my mouth and believe in my heart . . . and that's all?" She asked, with a hint of disbelief.

"That's how you start," I said.

She nodded. The features of her face combined in an expression of peace.

But when she read the Scripture again—in her mother tongue, instead of in English—her face changed.

"What's wrong?" I asked.

"It's just . . . so serious. I need to think about this more."

I accepted her hesitation. I was proud that she wasn't jumping lightly into a faith commitment. She knew the stakes. She understood.

We closed the book and I prayed for her to have peace with her decision. The warmth remained long after Chloe had left, long after my milk tea was gone. I was full of hope.

And I was feeling pretty successful, too.

Twenty-four hours later I walked through the campus rubbing my hands together in a futile effort to stave off the cold that stiffened my fingers like arthritis, my warm apartment a distant memory. The rest of my team was there, meeting for prayer and Bible study, but I had to escape.

So I walked.

My relationship with one particular teammate had deteriorated to the point that I no longer felt comfortable in the same room with him. So, instead of praying for Chloe with my co-laborers, I hustled around campus trying to keep my heart rate up, looking for a spot in the sun or out of the wind.

I sat down against the brick of a classroom wall and took out my journal. I tried to write out the mystery of what had happened between us. How had we let it get so bad?

Initially, when we rubbed each other the wrong way, we both just let it go. We didn't want to start a conflict over something small. But this pattern became a habit, and soon we were offending each other without knowing it, and our attempts to deal with our conflict grew less and less healthy.

One morning our leader gave a talk on evangelism from the parables. I thought it was a great talk, and so formative for my concept of evangelism. But my teammate didn't appear to receive any of our leader's wisdom—I could tell by his attitude and his facial expressions and his body language. I was offended on behalf of our leader, and I confronted my teammate, but by that point I was already angry (for conclusions I had drawn, based entirely on assumption). I was talking to him about his attitude in the session, but behind my words were the months of built-up frustration, so what came out was an overreaction.

I apologized later, but I kept handling our conflicts this way—waiting for the pressure to build, then letting it out negatively. For his part, he seemed to prefer denial. On the rare occasion that I brought up our conflict in a healthy way, he would deny it completely. He told me I must be the one with the problem, because he was at peace and had nothing against me. This statement didn't seem to line up with his words and actions, but I didn't know if he was lying to himself, or to me, or if he even saw it as a lie.

The cold in my bones drove the ability to grip a pen from my fingers. I stood up from the bricks that radiated their cold against my back, shoved my hands in my pockets, and continued my walk. My lungs filled up with cold air so that I shivered inside my thick jacket. After about fifteen minutes I found a warm patch of concrete in the sun. The light was fading as evening rose, but I took out my pen again to squeeze the last bit of ink from the situation.

After politeness, after anger and frustration, only guilt remained. I was so convicted by my failure to make the relationship work. I was driven from my own house by the presence of one who should have been my brother, and I felt so responsible for the situation.

When I prayed for him, I felt deep conviction. I knew he longed for acceptance, and my response should have been meekness and forgiveness. Standing on the idea of "my rights" was ridiculous in light of the fact that I'd laid them down in order to take up the cross. I was judging him in my heart instead of loving him. I was confronting him in anger rather than holding my tongue. I had made many, many mistakes.

And now it felt beyond repair. If he spoke to me at all, it was in a tone altogether different from the one he used to address everyone else. If he came into the room and saw me, his countenance fell. If I spoke in his presence, his eyes drifted off and his shoulders tensed up. He had become like a walking prison for me. So I ran.

Community is a powerful source in the life of a missionary.

I never sensed this power more than in the negativity I carried with me across the campus. Of course our team gatherings were unbearably tense, but I also stopped enjoying teaching. My private times with Jesus turned into times of mourning. Team meetings that should have bolstered my heart sucked the life out of me instead. The energy I should have been spending on loving my wife through her own difficult time was wasted going in circles in my head with my teammate. This single conflict, coupled with an identity based on ministry success, spread through every area of my life, settling in like a stiffening cold.

The sun fell and I couldn't sit there in the cold anymore. My hands weren't warming in my pockets. I walked slowly back home, pacing myself, hoping the meeting would be over by the time I arrived.

That such sweet hope for the salvation of my friend and such bitter conflict with my teammate could coexist within my conscious engine, propelling me through each day, may seem paradoxical, but we human beings are complex works of art.

Even as I ached with guilt and conviction and failure, my spirit soared with confidence in what God wanted for us.

We held another prayer vigil over the weekend, after I had extended the invitation for Chloe to become a Christ follower. Throughout the time of prayer I kept returning to the words of Isaiah about the new thing God would do—streams in the desert, water for the dry ground. At the flood of God's presence, all my internal garbage blessedly receded. I prayed so confidently for Chloe. I felt the power of God's words wash over me as he spoke his desire to bring in the harvest with a mighty hand.

During the vigil I recognized God's power in my own life as well, to raise me up from guilt and condemnation, to repair what seemed beyond repair. I prayed confidently for my teammate.

It seemed evident in that moment of prayer that God would do what he'd said he wanted to do. We all felt it. We all believed that our prayers for our students would be answered. His Spirit was, to us, a very present hope.

We wrapped up the prayer vigil in the morning, most of the tension between us having been scattered in the night—at least for the time being. We sang songs and encouraged one another to persist in hope. When my teammates left, I sat down to check my email. I excitedly opened a message from Chloe.

My excitement quickly faded when I read it.

She thanked me for studying with her, and talked about how she felt such peace around my family. She understood the invitation to follow Jesus, but she could not accept. She hid behind the traditions of her family as an excuse, and told me to understand that she would never be able to be counted as a Christian. Thanks anyway.

I sank into the couch, the same place we'd sat reading the Bible together for months, and I cried out my frustration to God. Why hadn't he moved? Why had he given me so much confidence and hope, and spoken so powerfully during our prayer vigil if she was never going to believe anyway?

He said, "You've been faithful with what I've asked you to do."

I said, "But I want her to believe!"

He said, "Yeah. Me, too."

Faith is a gift; it is also a choice.

God was speaking to Chloe's heart; she knew it, and I knew it. But the choice to follow Jesus still belonged to her. He would not force her to receive his gift, and neither could I.

I understood the gentleness of God, but I wept over the email all the same. It was as if the single candle burning in the cave had been snuffed out, and now I was alone, in the dark, but for a God I could not touch, who seemed incredibly far away.

Things came to a head after that. The brokenness in my marriage, my labor of evangelism, the pain from my past, the difficulty of cultural barriers, and my conflicts within community coalesced into a throbbing weight of failure. It pressed down into me, and I accepted it as my identity. I walked beneath it with my head down and my shoulders sagging. It was the only voice I could hear. I skated through meetings without participating; I prepared empty lessons and zoned out while teaching them. I stopped trying to love.

I was like a zombie.

One night I woke to the cries of my daughter. I went into her room to comfort her against the bad dreams. I wiped her tears, but they kept reappearing five or ten minutes later. I lay next to her, trying to soothe her in my wakefulness, only to have nightmares of my own when I drifted off to sleep—nightmares about how I failed over and over again, about how I was broken too badly to be fixed, about how heeding the call of God had been a terrible mistake.

I lay there most of the night, stroking my daughter's hair, huddling beneath the blankets for a distant memory of warmth, weeping my own tears and praying for God to come.

PART IV

Grace

sixteen

Phoenix

TINY STREAMS OF WATER peeled down the window as the bus made its way slowly through a light, Spring rain. I traced them with my index finger, lost in their lines and the songs in my headphones. I felt many things, but above the drone and turmoil of conflicting emotions one sentiment rose from the rest: I was grateful that things hadn't gone the way I'd planned.

Imagine what the disciples were feeling when Jesus was sleeping through the storm, how great the wind and the rain must have been to rattle the fishermen who did this for a living. They woke him when they reached the point of desperation, and he calmed the storm with such ease.[1] How safe they must have felt with Jesus after that!

Then they stepped off the boat and encountered the demon possessed man.[2] Imagine the terrible, inhuman voice of Legion speaking through the man's ravaged body. On the sea, the fishermen could handle themselves, at least to some degree. But these were much deeper waters. Here, in the presence of such evil, they were frightened again.

Jesus loved the dirty, scabbed man that everyone else relegated to the caves. Legion's power over the man was nothing compared

1. Mark 4:39.
2. Mark 5:1–20.

to Jesus. Imagine how it felt for the disciples to hear Legion cry out the identity of Christ, when they themselves had been questioned about their faith only the night before.

What was it like for that tormented man? He lived ashamed and in pain and utterly alone, wishing for death, and then his body was thrown at the feet of Jesus, and suddenly all the voices in his head receded, shrinking before the image of a carpenter. Then, instantly, he was free. Jesus helped him to his feet. Imagine how that peace and healing must have shocked his system.

I stared out the bus window, knowing this same deliverance had taken hold of me, too. I sensed God's sufficiency and his deep concern for me. I knew the foolishness of worry and strife as God asked, "Don't you know who I am?"

I felt the shadow that had grown over my life and ministry begin to crack.

Whether born into poverty or opulence, whether raised in the East or the West, every child of God is born a refugee.

We are born into an exiled family, children of wartime. We are born in trenches amidst gunfire and clouds of tear gas. We are born upon a wasteland of human death and decay, a battlefield littered with fire and bodies and blood. Refugees.

But we are born. We grow stronger. That we can survive at all is grace. That we can thrive in the midst of this battle is an outright miracle.

Like refugees, we all long for a home we can remember, though we've never quite known. In the West it can be hard for us to perceive the battlefield. We often can't see it, so comfortable as we make ourselves, but it is no less real. And to fight the battle we must take to heart the words of Psalm 108: "For vain is the salvation of man! With God we will do valiantly."[3]

The substance of my battle, at that point in time, was what I considered to be my cumulative failure in evangelism, community, and cultural acquisition. I had made that failure my identity. And

3. Ps 108:12b–13a.

deeper still, in tunnels beneath the battlefield, the demons from my past scurried back and forth, like enemy soldiers resupplying the lies I'd believed from childhood.

Jesus was my only hope.

His comfort came primarily from two Scriptures.

In John 14, Jesus tells his weary and fearful disciples that though he is going away, he is preparing a place for them,[4] and he will send them a helper.[5] In other words, he answers their fears by saying, "I'm only just ahead of you, getting something very good ready. And while I'm away, I'll send you an even better comforter, my Spirit, inside you."

The closeness of Jesus—like he was just ahead of me on the path—and the comfort of the Holy Spirit became harder and harder to ignore in my life.

Psalm 85 says, "Steadfast love and faithfulness meet. Righteousness and peace kiss each other. Faithfulness springs up from the ground, and righteousness looks down from the sky. Yes, the Lord will give what is good, and our land will yield its increase. Righteousness will go before him and make his footsteps a way."[6]

In one sense, these words are about how God deals with us— true and just, loving and intimate—causing his favor to fall on our land (and the soil of our hearts) so that it can produce a good crop, and his righteousness sweeps the path clean so that it becomes one we can follow. But in another sense, maybe a truer sense, this is about God in the person of Jesus—a kiss, an intimate meeting— speaking to one moment in time. Heaven and earth meet in the Christ. It is he who makes us bear fruit. His own righteousness makes his footsteps into a path—a way we can follow after him.

These two passages spoke a quiet hope to my soul. My circumstance had not changed. I was still downcast and beaten, and I spoke a kind of hatred over myself with frequency, but this hope was stirring: My circumstances were not the only reality. In fact, they were only a scrim, covering the truer reality of my identity.

4. John 14:2.
5. John 14:26.
6. Ps 85:10–13 ESV.

In the third chapter of Ephesians, Paul explains why he bows to pray for the followers of Christ: "That according to the riches of his glory he may grant you to be strengthened with power through his Spirit in your inner being."[7] We skip easily over these words because they've grown familiar to us, but imagine for a moment "the riches of his glory." His glory is immense. It is immeasurably huge. It is to this degree that our Father lavishes his forgiveness upon us, and grants us new identity—strength in our inmost being, and knowledge of his surpassing love.[8]

That I could read those words, and still find a way to condemn myself might seem incredible, but I found a way.

Everything was breaking my heart. I couldn't look at my wife and daughter without feeling intensely guilty. I felt the same about student work, and it drove me toward distraction. I watched a string of movies on my computer. Then I condemned myself for laziness and sloth. I was supposed to be an heir, not a slave. Paul would have been as perplexed by my attitude as he was by the Galatian church.[9]

On that rainy morning, my wife put me on the bus and told me to take the day off. She understood even better than I did how badly I needed the voice of Jesus to break through.

On the bus I watched the rain trace lines on the window, and I asked God how to cultivate a satisfaction with my life. I asked him to protect me as I took an honest look at myself. I appeared so wanting in my own eyes: a broken sinner, carrying the wreckage of his parents, lazy and selfish and dark. A failure.

I felt like a creep, but a creep for whom Jesus had traded his life.

Fathom this. He takes the inheritance I should receive and replaces it with his own. In the ashes of his death, and mine, I am reborn—a phoenix—a new creature born in ashes. It is not just a cloak that I wear; it is a fiery bird, his Spirit within me. The dirt on

7. Eph 3:16 ESV.
8. Eph 3:19 ESV.
9. Gal 3:1–4.

me is only the leftover image of my life in the shadows, the man I used to be, but am no longer.

I am new.

These thoughts filled my head, and I was desperate to believe that God was speaking them to me, teaching me his grace and calling out an identity I had claimed without ever really knowing it inside. As I prayed on the bus, I grew certain that I was in the throes of a spiritual paradigm shift. I was laying hold of my true identity.

I was baptized in my youth, I chose more decisively to follow Jesus in high school, I studied about him and traveled the world to serve him, I became a missionary—all without really understanding my true identity as a son of God. And that simple revelation changed me profoundly.

My circumstances were still hard, but I walked through them like a new man. The very next day I had an opportunity to test the reality of my new identity on the teammate with whom I was in deep conflict. He let on that I'd offended him, but continued to deny he had a problem, which would have sent me into a mental spiral of shadow arguments a week earlier. I was angry for a while, but when I went away and prayed, I rested in my identity, and an apology to that teammate came easily.

Loving my wife through her pregnancy took on a different tone. My work with students breathed new life (because I was more aware of the glory into which I was inviting them).

His grace, like rain, carved a new man from the old. I imagined myself rising from the ashes, like a phoenix.

To my surprise, Chloe continued to study the Bible with me. After making clear that she would never choose to follow Jesus, she was happy that I still wanted to be her friend. When I asked her if she wanted to continue to learn the Bible, she agreed.

Having reached the point of invitation—and her having rejected that invitation—I was unsure of exactly what to study with her. We looked at the lives of Paul and the disciples—men whose lives had been drastically changed by encounters with Jesus.

Chloe had made a decision, and she thought it was final. But the truer reality was that God was not finished pursuing her. As I prayed for her I heard the voice of the Lord speak so clearly: "It's not over."

My leaders prayed a prayer for me that clung to my bones for days afterward. They asked that I would receive healing from past scars, freedom to walk in the Spirit, and that walls that had hindered the presence of God in my life would topple. I felt the weight of his holiness rest upon me so heavily, so beautifully. I swelled with confidence—that he knew me, and I knew him, and that he chose me.

Quite literally, the shadow over me was cracking. The outline of a man I had ceased to be years before, held up by a scaffold of lies, was disintegrating. At the point of my deepest need on the mission field—when everything was broken, from my heart, to my community, to my ministry—God met me, and he lifted my head.

You might hear the same story from a dozen other missionaries. It is not uncommon. Yet, it is rarely the story we tell first. In order to get to the truth of who you are, you have to pass through some pain. If you want to be used by God, you have to be willing to let him build you into the right tool for the job.

We don't talk about this in the brochures or on the websites or when we're giving recruitment speeches to rooms full of students. Maybe we don't talk about it because it's long, and we're afraid people might lose interest. Maybe we think our audience can't hang on through the painful part in the middle, long enough to reach the beautiful conclusion God is working toward. Or maybe we don't talk about it because we're ashamed to be too vulnerable. Maybe we think the stories of our transformation are too personal, and that people might think we're self-absorbed if we tell them, and we should just stick to testimonies of miracles and revivals and conversions.

But the truth is that this is the story of everyone who lays down a life for Jesus.

We are all like the phoenix, born from Christ's death; alive with fire.

I went off the edge of the map to serve God, and he met me there, and he healed me.

I wrote these words on the front of a new journal:

All praise be to my God—my Father, and my friend—and my Lord, Jesus, who bore my sin and death, and gave me a new life, which I now live on wings of fire.

To this day, hope remains.

seventeen

Resolved

My wife will have our new baby next week. We still don't know if we're having a boy or a girl. All the doctors and nurses in our hometown are unaccustomed to delivering surprises, so they seem extra excited, which makes us extra excited.

Last night I sat on the porch of my father-in-law's house and I talked to my wife about the future. We considered all the potential reasons to abandon our two-year commitment. Pregnancy, after all, had never been part of the contract. We took stock of the pros and cons of living overseas, and trying to raise an infant amidst a culture in which we ourselves felt like infants. We made lists: to go home, or to stay the course.

Halfway through the list we opened our laptop to look at pictures of our going-away party.

Our students had thrown my wife and daughter a surprise party the week before we went back to America. They decorated our building with lights and hung up a huge banner. They brought food and cakes and presents. We played games and they all sang us a song together.

We looked at the pictures of the smiling faces of our students, and the smiles bursting from our own faces, and the face of our daughter. We saw how happily she played with them, and the joy in their eyes as they lifted her into the sky. We saw how much they loved us, and we realized how we had grown to love them.

We missed our students. We missed our teammates. We had grown so accustomed to life together that life back in America left us feeling lonely and wanting.

We laughed about my wife's trips to the hospital—fighting her way through crowds of sick people murmuring words she couldn't understand, sticking her arm through what looked like a bank teller's window to give blood, and how they never failed to get her vein on the first try. We compared those trips to the U.S. hospitals we'd recently visited, one of which turned us down because our medical records were written in a foreign language.

We took our daughter to an American fast-food restaurant for her favorite snack—chicken nuggets—and she asked if we could go home soon, where they had her kind of chicken nuggets.

Even our daughter thought of that place as home.

We resolved, in our hearts, to go back.

I want to be clear in stating that though we are on our way to wholeness, we aren't there yet. Our marriage is still far from perfect. Anger and bitterness still reside in my heart where there should be patience and satisfaction. My wife says that fear and grumbling still plague the places inside her where there ought to be trust and thankfulness. The ghosts in my past occasionally haunt my waking days, and sometimes my dreams, as well. We still can't speak the language, we still don't understand the culture, and people still get on our nerves.

We are not perfect, but neither are we sidelined.

God uses the weak things of the world to confound the strong. We will continue to serve him in our weakness, and there will be no question as to whom glory is due.

When we go back to the place my daughter calls home, we will again be weak and witless, unsure of how to care for an infant in a foreign country. We will again be wading the murky waters, shallow in places, deep in others.

We can't wait to see the ways God will show up.

When I shut my eyes to pray, no matter what I had intended to pray about, I pray for Chloe. I pray that God will break through in her life with such a revelation of his goodness that she will be unable to resist him, and choose to give him her life.

Maybe I finally understand those missionaries who came to my church, who seemed to love the people and culture with such passion. I don't feel that way about everything and everyone in the country where I work, but without question I feel it about Chloe. She hijacks every prayer I lift.

My journey off the edge of the map was imperfect, yet ordained.

The life which I lead off the edge of the map is messy, and it is also holy.

I will face trials, and I will see his glory. I will hope continually, and I will praise him yet, more and more.

These are the things God did with a single year of my life, the transformations he set in motion. What might he do in yours if you were to follow him off the edge of the map?

Acknowledgments

PILGRIM TYNE WOULD LIKE to thank his supportive wife, who contributed a great deal to this project and who never uttered a single complaint after her first year abroad; his daughters, who continually demonstrate the blessing of God in his life; Megan and Gayle, who read his manuscript and offered kind and honest feedback which was taken to heart; the supporters (financial and otherwise) who keep him and his family serving on the mission field; and finally, his teammates (year one and beyond) from whose lives and stories he is privileged to draw.

Bibliography

Atallah, Ramez. "The Scandal of the Incarnation." Urbana 09. America's Center, St. Louis, MO, 27 Dec. 2009.

Evert, Don, and Doug Schaupp. *I Once Was Lost*. Illinois: IVP Books, 2008.

Franklin, John. "Building the Artist: A Spiritual Foundation." Urbana 09. America's Center, St. Louis, MO, 28 Dec. 2009.

Foster, Richard. *Prayer: Finding the Heart's True Home*. San Francisco: Harper Collins, 1992.

Fung, Patrick. Interview by Greg Jao. Urbana 09. America's Center, St. Louis, MO, 28 Dec. 2009.

Keller, Timothy. "The Community of Jesus." Timothy Keller Podcast. 10 Feb. 2010. Retrieved from: www.itunes.com.

Lee, Li-Young, "This Room and Everything in it." *The City in Which I Love You*. New York: BOA Editions, Ltd. 1990.

Moore, York. "Vision of Another World." Urbana 09. America's Center, St. Louis, MO, 30 Dec. 2009.

Muriu, Oscar. Message Given at Urbana 09. Urbana 09. America's Center, St. Louis, MO, 29 Dec. 2009.

Paul, Nigel. Speech Given at Urbana 09 Seminar: Birthing Missional Communities on the Field. Urbana 09. America's Center, St. Louis, MO, 29 Dec. 2009.

Spafford, Horatio. "It is Well With my Soul." 1873. Retrieved from: http://library.timelesstruths.org/music/It_Is_Well_with_My_Soul/.